The Soul of Elizabeth Seton

Joseph I. Dirvin, C.M.

The Soul of Elizabeth Seton

IGNATIUS PRESS   SAN FRANCISCO

Cover art by Katie Osenga
Cover design by Roxanne Mei Lum

With ecclesiastical approval
© 1990 Ignatius Press, San Francisco
All rights reserved
ISBN 0-89870-269-0
Library of Congress catalogue number 89-83260
Printed in the United States of America

C1

CONTENTS

PREFACE

This contemplation of a great Christian soul is the result of thirty years of research, study, meditation, writing and lecturing. Thankfully, it seems an endless process. The depths of St. Elizabeth Ann Seton's spirituality remain unsounded; the facets of her personality and character continue to reveal themselves; her endless attractiveness is ever drawing new friends and clients. The effect of her life and holiness on the lives and holiness, and indeed the salvation, of generations of religious daughters, intimate devotees and the whole body, past and present, of American Catholics stands evident and shining before the universal Church and society. I have the personal experience of how benevolently she has changed my life as proof of how she has changed, and continues to change, the lives of countless others.

It is the purpose of this extended reflection on the spirituality of St. Elizabeth Ann to further still her influence on other souls. We shall never know the glorious reaches of her perfection in God, but we can guess at them, at least, through her own unwitting revelations of heroic virtue. It is to authenticate these revelations that I have allowed her to disclose them in her own words, certified by footnotes and citations, lest they be thought of as wishful fantasies of the author's imagination.

Certain citations appear more than once, usually under different circumstances and for different purposes. Citations have not been edited or tampered with, except for obvious lapses in grammar, slight changes—for the sake of clarity—in punctuation and, in a few instances, spelling and the adoption of a uniform system of capitalization (even awkward or archaic usages have been retained). They have been rigorously checked and rechecked against the originals in the saint's own hand or those of her friends and correspondents.

7

The rock on which St. Elizabeth Ann Seton's spirituality was built was that special attention to the Person and Model of Jesus Christ characteristic of the great spiritual masters of the seventeenth century — St. Francis de Sales, Cardinal de Bérulle, Charles de Condren, St. Vincent de Paul. This Christocentric approach to perfection was further refined by the personalities and callings of individuals. Thus it came to St. Elizabeth Ann Seton through the minute attention to Christ and love for the poor and the clergy of Vincent de Paul; the preoccupation with sacred training of his disciple Jean-Jacques Olier, the founder of the Sulpicians, who were her directors; its feminine interpretation by St. Louise de Marillac, who had also been influenced in her early years by the Capuchins Honoré de Champigny, Ange de Joyeuse and Bênoit de Canfield; and, of course, the familiar but profound teaching of Francis de Sales and his co-worker Baroness de Chantal — it was no accident that Simon Gabriel Bruté likened Elizabeth Seton's soul to that of St. Jane Francis de Chantal — both of whom were friends and spiritual idols of St. Vincent and St. Louise. (It is for this reason that a generous sprinkling of books available in English concerning Vincent and Louise has been included in the Bibliography.)

Mrs. Seton was certainly drawn to the Person of Christ in her Episcopalian worship and, of course without knowing it, to the Vincentian apostolate to the poor and to children by her work with the Widow's Society. Thus she took quite naturally to the type of religious life suggested to her by Sulpician Father William Valentine Dubourg: "In her frequent conferences with her director [himself]," he has testified, "Mrs. Seton learned that he had thought for a long time of establishing the Daughters of Charity in America; and as the duties of this institute would be compatible with the cares of her family, this virtuous lady expressed a most ardent desire of seeing it commenced and of being herself admitted into it." When Elizabeth had read the Rule of these same Daughters, she had "not a thought discordant" with it. Among her first gifts to her infant community were her own translations of the lives of St. Vincent and St. Louise.

This innate and committed Christocentrism of Elizabeth Seton should, therefore, be kept constantly in mind while studying her soul in the following pages.

I am grateful to Sister Elizabeth Ann Tonroe, D.C., former assistant and counselor for formation, Emmitsburg Province of the Daughters of Charity, whose invitation to mark the 175th anniversary of Mother Seton's Community with a series of lectures on the saint's unique spirituality led to this work; to her and to Father John J. Lawlor, C.M., director of the same Province, and Father William J. Casey, C.M., for their wise comments and suggestions; to Sister Aloysia Dugan, D.C., provincial archivist, for her invaluable knowledge of sources and wholehearted assistance; and to all the Sisters of St. Joseph's Provincial House, as well as my Vincentian confreres of Emmitsburg's St. Vincent's House, for their hospitality and interest.

May God, our common father St. Vincent de Paul, and St. Elizabeth Ann Seton reward them all.

Joseph I. Dirvin, C.M.

Mother Elizabeth Ann Bayley Seton. (This portrait was painted for the Filicchi family, an engraving of Mother Seton being used for the face, and the habit painted around it.)

I

"SHE IS A SAINT"

The announcement by Pope Paul VI, on December 12, 1974, that Elizabeth Ann Seton would be canonized during the Holy Year of 1975 brought, besides the satisfaction and joy of millions of American Catholics, some curious responses. A priest asked whether she was being canonized because she was a foundress of the American parochial school.[1] A nun, one of her own religious daughters, expressed her distaste for the pomp and circumstance of the approaching event as "unnecessary, since we already know she is a saint".[2] A syndicated columnist in Catholic newspapers dismissed canonization as "just [recognizing] that some person had demonstrated exceptional qualities in life . . . worthy of imitation", thought that the local episcopal conference could handle it anyway without going "to Rome", wondered whether the "now generation" might not think a 150-year-old saint "just a little quaint", and was disappointed that "one more religious" was being canonized.[3]

All three displayed various degrees of ignorance concerning the nature of canonization. The priest should have known that people are canonized not for what they do but for what they are, not for the greatest and most enduring of accomplishments but for extraordinary personal holiness. The nun should have known that, despite the grace given her and her colleagues to know the appealing sanctity of Mother Seton, millions of their fellow Catholics in the nation and the world did not know what they knew, and the Church was most anxious that they should, for their own spiritual benefit. The columnist was the least informed of all. Canonization is profoundly related to the dogma that saints are to be venerated and invoked. It is the theologically certain teaching of the Church that the canonization of a saint is an infallible and irrevocable decision of the supreme Pontiff by which he also imposes a precept on the faithful of the Universal Church to venerate the person canonized with all the saints.[4] The infallible intention of the act is plain in the formula used to proclaim it, which is essentially the same as the formula for *ex cathedra* definitions of Catholic dogma. Thus, on Sunday, September 14, 1975, Pope Paul VI proclaimed:

> For the honor of the Most Holy Trinity, for the exaltation of the Catholic Faith and the increase of the Christian life, by the authority of Our Lord Jesus Christ, of the holy Apostles Peter and Paul and by Our authority, after mature deliberation and most frequent prayer for divine assistance, having obtained the counsel of many of our brother bishops, we declare and we define that Blessed Elizabeth Ann Bayley Seton is a saint, and we inscribe her name in the calendar of saints, and mandate that she should be devoutly honored among the saints in the universal Church.[5]

The Holy Father then expounded the theology of canonization with great precision in the first paragraphs of his homily. "Yes, venerable brothers and beloved sons and daughters," he began, "Elizabeth Ann Seton is a saint. We rejoice and we are deeply moved that our apostolic ministry authorizes us to make this solemn declaration before all of you here present, before the Holy Catholic Church, before the entire American people, and before all humanity. Elizabeth Ann Bayley Seton is a saint." It is the Pope's apostolic office as successor of St. Peter that gives him the authority to canonize; his pronouncement is universal, to the whole Church and to all the world, and it is now part of the Church's Magisterium, or teaching. "The Church", he continued, "has made this study of the life, that is, the interior and exterior history, of Elizabeth Ann Seton. And the Church has exulted with admiration and joy and has today heard her own charism of truth poured out in the exclamation that we send up to God and announce to the world: she is a saint."

Having thus established the authenticity of the teaching, the Pope then set it in the context of the transcendent doctrines of the Church as Christ's Mystical Body and the communion of saints: "This will be one of the most valuable fruits of the canonization of the new saint: to know her, in order to admire in her an outstanding human figure, in order to praise God, who is wonderful in His saints, to imitate her example, which this ceremony places in a light that will give perennial edification, to invoke her protection"—Elizabeth Seton now has awesome power: to influence her fellow creatures to salvation by the power of her example and to speak for them before God's throne by the power of intercession—"now that we have the certitude of her participation in the exchange of heavenly life in the Mystical Body of Christ, which we call the communion of saints and in which we also share, although still belonging to life on earth."[6]

The "now generation" may very well be unimpressed by many things because no one ever took the trouble to teach them what they have a right to know. Men and women dead for centuries have enormous influence on today's world. Rousseau's wrongheaded doctrine of hedonism is still widely accepted and practiced. A great saint like Vincent de Paul still inspires millions of people, priests, religious and laity, who perpetuate his abundant charity—to say nothing of his impact on social work and workers who may never have heard of him. He had a decided influence on Elizabeth Seton. As for saints of bygone days bursting on the modern world, it is a fact of history that God gives the Church and the world the saints they need at a particular time. It is true that many of the saints provided for various crises were alive during them; that God gives these critical days a saint dead for more than 150 years is significant in itself. Many of the Jews of Jesus' day failed to recognize Him because they were looking for a different kind of Messiah than the One who came.

Elizabeth Seton had the kind of simple, serene faith, unfaltering hope and practical love of God and man the modern world needs desperately. She had total dedication to God, Church and country, to family, to the poor, to the sick and the old, to the priesthood, to the religious life, to the Christian education of the young—to so many things that continue in crisis today. She was, indeed, a religious, the foundress of the first American religious community, but for only twelve of her forty-six years. A laywoman for thirty-four years, she was a Protestant laywoman for thirty of them. Even her religious vocation was for the laity, as she told her young pupils, not "to teach you how to be good nuns or Sisters of Charity, but . . . to fit you for that world in which you are destined to live: to teach you how to be good . . . mothers of families".[7]

Archbishop (now Cardinal) Joseph Bernardin, then president of the American National Conference of Catholic Bishops, chose to address this very timeliness of Mother Seton's canonization. In thanking the Holy Father "on behalf of the bishops, clergy, religious and Catholic people of the United States" for his gift of the new saint, the Archbishop insisted that she

> did not live long ago and far away. She died a little over 150 years ago. New York, Baltimore and the Maryland countryside were the setting for her work and growth in holiness. She was a wife and mother, a religious sister and educator, a woman who faced crises and setbacks which she surmounted by love, devotion and openness to the grace of God. In proclaiming her a saint, the Church invites each of us to respond like her to the challenges in our own life.
>
> She was an American religious and foundress of a religious community, and she remains a model for religious today. She was the "mother" of the Catholic school system in the United States, whose efforts underline the importance of the educational apostolate. She was a Roman Catholic whose spiritual life was nourished by long membership in the Episcopal Church. The coming-together in her of two great Christian traditions is an inspiration to contemporary work for Christian unity.[8]

The late Cardinal John Wright, prefect of the Sacred Congregation of the Clergy, discussed the significance of St. Elizabeth Ann's canonization as it related to her native land. "Why do we Americans rejoice in the canonization of this particular saint," he asked,

> even while insisting, if our theology is straight, that while there may be a saintly American, there is no such thing as an *American* saint and while there may be and assuredly are many Americans who are saints, there are no *saints* who depend on their *Americanism* or *Gallicanism* or *Orientalism* for their sanctity? It merely means— *but this means very much* —that while her nationality may or may not contribute to the essence of her sanctity, her sanctity does very much for her nationality and if we had enough citizens like her, her nation would become indeed a holy place as well as the beautiful and admirable place we know it to be.

The Cardinal then proceeded to expand on the true and wondrous universality now attained by this little woman who had ended her days in the isolated woods and mountains of Maryland—a universality extending itself first to her fellow citizens and then to all the world. "Our mass media . . . headlines the news that now the Church has an *American* saint, whereas the fact is that America has a canonized saint who is the symbol of the millions of uncanonized saints who go to work or tend their homes or suffer in their hospitals or do their good works or beg the help of their neighbors all over the United States."

"It does not mean", the Cardinal reiterated, "that the Church recognizes that a Catholic convert has 'made good' by American standards; it means that an American wife, mother, educator, religious, convert to Catholicism and heroic woman has 'made good' by God's much more exacting standards. It is ample reason for *American* rejoicing but it is a cause for universal joy in the Church throughout the world and in heaven itself."[9]

No matter what Elizabeth Seton did, however, or how well, or in what land, she attained sainthood only by complete union with God. "Being a saint means being perfect", Paul VI reminded us, "with a perfection that attains the highest level that a human being can reach." But this perfection is attained only because

> a saint is a human creature fully conformed to the will of God. A saint is a person in whom all sin—the principle of death—is canceled out and replaced by the living splendor of divine grace.
>
> The analysis of the concept of sanctity brings us to recognize in a soul that mingling of two elements that are entirely different, but which come together to produce a single effect: sanctity. One of these elements is the human and moral element, raised to the degree of heroism; heroic virtues are always required by the Church for the recognition of a person's sanctity. The second element is the mystical element, which expresses the measure and form of divine action in the person chosen by God to realize in herself—always in an original way—the image of Christ.[10]

These elements are surely recognizable in the pains Elizabeth took to do all things well, whether attendance at Mass or the daily running of her school, despite the steady downpull of illness, as well as in the ecstatic, sometimes nearly wild and incoherent, love poured out in her private spiritual jottings and notes to her director.

It is indeed true, as Paul VI has remarked, that "the science of sanctity is . . . the most interesting, the most varied, the most surprising and the most fascinating of all the studies of that ever mysterious being which is man".[11] It is the very humanity of saints that makes it so, for shared as humanity is by all, its manifestations are as varied as are men and women. Conversely, it is also true that the humanity in the people of God seeks out the humanity in the saints and is consequently attracted to, indifferent to or repelled by them. Thus there are very few modern Christians who are drawn to the austerity of the desert fathers, but there are myriads drawn to the delightful personality of Elizabeth Ann Seton. She was pleasant, loving, wise and witty, even mischievous; however, she was also long-suffering, brave, disciplined and relentless for the truth in herself and others. She cannot be wholly embraced, she cannot be truly loved or effectively admired—indeed, she can do little good—unless souls drawn to her accept the two elements of her sanctity, the human and moral, and the mystical.

Fortunately, Elizabeth herself so commingled these elements that they were the warp and the woof of her daily life. They appear in startling juxtapositions—family events with holy indignation, the divine and the trivial—but without jostling or jarring. Elizabeth's letters are filled with examples of this saintly dexterity. Thus she wrote to her dear Filicchi in sympathy and reminder, "When thought goes to you, Antonio, and imagines you in the promiscuous company you must meet, without any solid gratification, fatigued by your excursions, wandering in your fancy, etc.—oh! how I pray that the Holy Spirit may not leave you, and that your dear angel may even pinch you at the hour of prayer rather than suffer you to neglect them."[12] To this same Antonio, whom she could tease mercilessly, she could also be frank in affection because her affection was fastened in God. "I could cry out now, as my poor Seton used to: 'Antonio, Antonio, Antonio'," she wrote in the same letter, "but call back the thought and my soul cries out: 'Jesus, Jesus, Jesus!' There it finds rest and heavenly peace, and is hushed by that dear sound as my little babe is quieted by my cradle song." Is there any more beautiful expression of earthly and divine love, any more profound sublimation of the one to the other, nay, holy merging of the two? "Jonathan loved David as his own soul," she continued in the same mystical vein, "and if I was your brother, Antonio, I would never leave you for one hour. But, as it is, I try rather to turn every affection to God, well knowing that there alone their utmost exercise cannot be misapplied, and most ardent hopes can never be disappointed."[13] This letter is not only sublime but also most important, for it goes to the heart of Elizabeth Seton, which was wholly affectionate and loving. She loved her family and friends with a passionate intensity that could easily have obscured and usurped her love of God. This letter confirms that it did not, and why. She knew the joys of love and friendship, but she also knew the priorities of salvation and perfection, and she managed both carefully and well. This balance extended to every sphere of life. For example, the following lines, written to Amabilia Filicchi on the day of Elizabeth's reception into the Catholic Church, are a delightful melange of good-humored exasperation, profound adoration and union and maternal happiness:

> For as to going a-walking any more about what all the different people believe, I cannot, being quite tired out—and I came up light at heart and cool of head the first time these many long months—but not without begging Our Lord to wrap my heart deep in that opened side so well described in the beautiful Crucifixion,* or lock it up in His little tabernacle, where I shall now rest forever. Oh, Amabilia, the endearments of this day with the children, and the play of the heart with God while keeping up their little farces with them![13]

One of the happy by-products of Elizabeth's grasp of the complex interweaving of the earthly and heavenly, the human and divine, was the way she could talk about the profoundly spiritual in the homeliest of terms, thus putting it in the reach of all, as God intended. As her strength ebbed away in her last years, she once wrote to a young priest she had befriended from the day he entered the seminary, "I cannot die one way, it seems, so I try to die the other, and keep the straight path to God alone. The little daily lesson: to keep soberly and quietly in His Presence, trying to turn every little action on His Will; and to praise and love through cloud and sunshine is all my care and study. *Sam* offers his battle from time to time"—Sam was her own nickname for the devil—"but Our Beloved stands behind the wall and keeps the wretch his distance. So much for your Mother's little nothing part; but oh," she urged, "mind your own, so great and glorious, for whether in action or at rest you are forever *His priest*".[15]

No one knows a soul better than a spiritual director. In a sense, he knows the soul of his penitent better than his own, because he has a more objective view of it. After Elizabeth Seton's death, her director, Father Simon Gabriel Bruté, had this to say of her: "I would say from the bottom of my heart, out of conviction from

---

* A painting by Vallejo in St. Peter's Church.

long and intimate acquaintance, that I believe hers was one of those elite souls, with the like characteristics found in St. Teresa and St. Jane Frances de Chantal, just as capable of as unbelievable a holiness, it being impossible to find similar or greater elevation, purity and love of God, heaven, supernatural and eternal things than were found in her."[16]

This is an authoritative and uncompromising testimonial to Elizabeth Seton's sanctity, but one perhaps more authentic, because more personal, more moving. Bruté confided to his private journal (in the broken and awkward English that gave Elizabeth such mischievious delight) on May 19, 1821:

O my mother, be blessed in heaven of hope already!

Many times pressed to write of you, this morning, at least this line of my conviction how sincerely holy, elevated, humbly kind, merciful, eager to do good, attached to faith, loving your Jesus, ardent for His presence in the Eucharist you were—what a mind, a heart, a soul I have known and enjoyed, and now removed—oh, my whole life to remember you and cherish the remembrance—how much of grace I have received by you— you said you did by me, but how rather, alas! How do I regret the many pains, many acts of indiscreet zeal, reproof, request, trouble I was guilty with you—one good may be from it, O good, good God, was to keep you the better attached to Him alone—and indeed to Him alone I wanted to give you with the same horror of self you had. . . .

Mother, how pleased I feel to have written some lines!—alas! foolish, if not to feed my heart and renew impressions which drew me so forcibly to my God—my God, my God, Thou alone![17]

Meditation on the Desire of Death

Consider that it is a great grace not to be afraid of Death: and it is a great perfection to desire it with a well regulated desire according to God — — for what Virtue can the soul possess which is not contained in the Desire of death? it possesses Humility since it is ready to recieve all the humiliations of death, to return to dust & corruption,., it possesses Poverty, since it is ready to quit all that the world contains, and chastity since it turns from all its joys & pleasures

Oh the happiness of a poor exile entering his home, and the house of his family, .. ol the embrace of his Father, and the welcome of his friends !!!

I consider a good Death as the passage from death to life — the life of this world is truly a death, by dying we find life, and lose Death ;, and by this loss how immense, is our gain !!! —

come then O Death! that I may no more offend my god, no more oppose his Will, — come take my soul deliver it from this wretched frailty which makes it fall so often, and for what is in itself nothing. — come, Goddesire you, desire you with my whole heart.

2

"... AND THEN ETERNITY"

Eternity was the motivation of Elizabeth Seton's life and perfection. It was an all-embracing word to her. It meant more than the next world's lasting forever. It meant God and happiness and reunion with loved ones.

Even when Elizabeth was a small child, eternity was never far from her thoughts. Granted, it was not the encompassing vision of her later years, but the elements were there in the simple, uncomplicated turning to God and longing for her mother, who had died when Elizabeth was a toddler.

Elizabeth recalled when she was only four, "sitting alone on a step of the door, looking at the clouds, while my little sister Catherine, two years old, lay in her coffin; they asked me: Did I not cry when little Kitty was dead? No, because Kitty is gone up to heaven. I wish I could go, too, with Mama."[1] She recalled a year or so later carrying her baby half-sister Emma up to the topmost window of the house to watch the sunset and telling the infant very solemnly that "God lived up in heaven, and good children would go up there".[2] At her Uncle William Bayley's country seashore home in New Rochelle, where she spent much of her childhood because of the neglect of her busy father and indifferent stepmother, "every little leaf and flower, or animal, insect, shades of clouds, or waving trees" became "objects of vacant unconnected thoughts of God and heaven"[3] to the little eight-year-old, who also found it a "delight to sit alone by the waterside, wandering hours on the shore, humming and gathering shells"—and again—"thoughts of God and heaven".[4]

It is obvious that even in these tenderest years Elizabeth had grasped the basic truth that "we have not here a lasting city, but seek one that is to come".[5] She had undoubtedly learned it in a child's unquestioning way from her minister grandfather, the Reverend Richard Charlton, and his daughter Catherine, Elizabeth's pious mother. Yet, seen from hindsight, there was more to it than that. That she absorbed this truth more deeply than a lesson learned by rote and that it pleased and attracted her and early became a guiding force are evidence of the plan of God, who was Himself at the time—it is not too much to say—her spiritual guide. This doting on eternity was an integral part of a burgeoning spirituality, unusual in one so young. She has testified that she had "pleasure in learning anything pious";[6] it is significant that Elizabeth's lone childhood recollection of her stepmother was that she "learnt me the twenty-second Psalm: 'The Lord is my shepherd, the Lord ruleth me. . . . Though I walk in the midst of the shadow of death, I will fear no evil, for thou art with me'; and all life through it has been the favorite Psalm."[7] This is quite understandable, because the Psalm's teaching was the compass of her whole spirituality.

This early, extraordinary absorption in the things of God gave rise to a series of teenage religious experiences, the first of which has all the earmarks of true contemplation: "In the year 1789"— Elizabeth was, then, not yet fifteen—

> when my father was in England, one morning in May, in the lightness of a cheerful heart, I jumped in the wagon that was driving to the woods for brush, about a mile from home; the boy who drove it began to cut, and I set off in the woods, soon found an outlet in a meadow; and a chestnut tree with several young ones growing around it, found rich moss under it and a warm sun. Here, then, was a sweet bed—the air still, a clear blue vault above—the numberless sounds of spring melody and joy— the sweet clovers and wildflowers I had got by the way, and a heart as innocent as human heart could

be, filled even with enthusiastic love to God and admiration of his works."[8]

A quarter of a century later, when Elizabeth recorded the event, it is still so vivid that she can see and delight in, as it were, every blade of grass. What is so extraordinary is her unaffected and mature judgment at the age of fifteen, when a young girl is awakening to the world and the vapors of romance are distorting reality. Hers was "a heart as innocent as human heart could be"; nor was it an innocuous innocence, an empty naïveté; no, that heart was "filled even with enthusiastic love to God and admiration of his works".

Elizabeth continues: "God was my father, my all. I prayed, sang hymns, cried, laughed, talking to myself of how far He could place me above all sorrow. Then I laid still to enjoy the heavenly peace that came over my soul; and I am sure, in the two hours so enjoyed, grew ten years in the spiritual life."[9] This considered judgment, made in experienced religious hindsight, is most extraordinary of all. Quite calmly, Elizabeth is recognizing genuine union with God with all its "signs and wonders", the *silent* prayer, after all the hymns and crying and babbling, however well meant, the mutual gazing of God and creature, the all-pervading peace, the permanent spiritual growth. It is possible to trace the ultimate source of this awesome spiritual event to Elizabeth's happy addiction to spiritual reading, especially the Holy Bible. Among her voluminous writings preserved at Emmitsburg, there are page after page of favorite Psalms meticulously and lovingly copied in her youthful Protestant years. Surely "the heart as innocent as human heart could be", the "enthusiastic love to God" and the "admiration of his works" are authentic echoes of the threads of praise binding these Psalms together. To the Bible Elizabeth added the religious poetry of authors such as John Milton and James Thomson, whose *The Seasons* Haydn has set to glorious music, but it was the Bible that ruled her mind, her life and her teaching.

Elizabeth's second fateful experience occurred two years later, when she was seventeen. It was at the opposite end of the scale from the first—it seems to have been the ultimate temptation to self-destruction—and yet was undoubtedly related to and even, however remotely, caused by that first ecstatic glimpse of God face to face. More than enough young people, especially in our desperate times, are tempted to suicide, and indeed an alarming number succumb. Depression is no stranger to the young years of confusion. Elizabeth's unusual involvement with God and the things of the spirit, however, bids us look deeper into the nature of her supreme temptation. There are no sure indications of what precipitated it; perhaps on the threshold of adulthood she began to feel truly the malevolence of her lack of family life and love, and there were the usual feverish absurdities to complicate growing up. She recorded in her *Dear Remembrances:* "16 years of age—family disagreement—could not guess why when I spoke kindly to relations they did not speak to me—could not even guess how anyone could be an enemy to another—folly—sorrows—romance, miserable friendships . . . " It is all very unsatisfactory, but also endlessly suggestive. At any rate, when the dark night came—and that it was some form of that dark night of the soul visited on privileged friends of God is more than probable, because of both Elizabeth's already advanced piety and her attempts to justify herself with Him—its threat of eternal darkness was very real: "Alas, alas, alas! *Tears of Blood* —" she recalled with stark vividness, "My God!—horrid subversion of every good promise of God in the boldest presumption—God had created me—I was very miserable. He was too good to condemn so poor a creature made of dust, driven by misery this the wretched reasoning—Laudanum—the praise and thanks of excessive joy not to have done the horrid deed, the thousand promises of eternal gratitude."[10] That she had definitely considered death as a surcease of sorrow is borne out in a letter written years later to her brother-in-law Henry Seton, who had asked whether it was wrong of him to wish he had not survived a shipwreck; she recalled in answer "the moment twenty years ago in which I asked myself the same question, dictated by that anguish of soul which can find no relief".[11] Other dark nights were to descend upon her, but none evoked the same panic, which was the natural lot of a young heart. Even so, the conquering faith and love were also there to rout the horror, to spare her the sad fate of so many empty young hearts in today's empty world.

Elizabeth's third teenage "experience" was really her awakening to a truth that many good-intentioned people have encountered before and since: that the world and the spiritual life do not mix very well. Elizabeth was a lively, outgoing girl, loving all the good things of life, dancing, horseback riding, skating parties on the frozen Hudson and East rivers, the theatre; but, at eighteen, she puzzled over a new awareness—"after being at public places, why I could not say my prayers and have good thoughts as if I had been at home".[12] It was her first taste of the distracting power of even the most innocent diversions. It was really not a problem for her because she was already "astonished at people's care in dress, in this world, etc.", thought "how silly" it was "to love anything in this world", and "preferred going to my room to amusement out of it".[13] Nevertheless, problem or not, and with every best intention and resolution, she would be a long time attaining life in but not of the world in all its absolute purity; it could only come gradually, with practice in subduing the natural attraction to innocent pleasures in favor of its usefulness for soul and body.

With the settling influence of her marriage to William Seton and the carrying of her first child, Elizabeth's motivation of eternity returned in full force. It had not yet the purity of later years, dwelling instead on the natural human fear of eternal punishment—as she herself was aware in later recollection, which could still recall the bewildered ecstasy of the new young wife: "My own home at 20—the world—that and heaven too—quite impossible! So every moment clouded with that fear: 'My God, if I enjoy this, I lose You'—yet no thought of who [sic] I would lose, rather fear of hell and shut out of heaven."[14] It was the uncomprehending cry of the soul in Francis Thompson's *Hound of Heaven*, "Lest having Him I must have naught beside",[15] and it would terrorize her until she understood the meaning of God in everything and everything in God. It was love, but imperfect love; the fear of loss surely bespoke love, but the wary, half-given love, the love that elicits the imperfect sorrow of the familiar Act of Contrition, dread of "the loss of heaven and the pains of hell"; she was not yet ready to say, "but, most of all, because [sin] offends you, my God".

After Elizabeth had gone through the purgation of her husband's last illness and death and her own conversion to the Catholic Faith and had entered upon the religious life, she was able to lift the clouding fear and recognize the unassailable love beneath it. "For my part, I find so much contentment in this love [of God]", she then told Julia Scott,

> that I am obliged to put on my consideration cap to find out how anyone can raise their eyes to the light of heaven and be insensible to it. I remember when Anna was six months old and everything smiled around me—venerating the virtues of my Seton and sincerely attached to him, accustomed to the daily visits and devoted love of my father, and possessed of all I estimated as essential to happiness—alone with this babe in the see-saw of motherly love, frequently the tears used to start and often overflowed, and I would say to myself while retrospecting the favors of heaven: "All these, these and heaven, too?"[16]

There is no mistaking the true love of God of this young wife and mother. The only things lacking are the peace and calm that drive out fear, the peace and calm that recognize the certainty of love, indeed, are that love's ultimate reward, the peace and calm that see no use for the desperate proofs to which Elizabeth still drove herself.

"Sometimes falling on my knees with the sleeping suckling in my arms, I would offer her and all my dear possessions—husband, father, home—and entreat the Bountiful Giver to separate me from all, if indeed I could not possess my portion here—and with Him, too." The offer was as honest as it was habitual: "Nor do I remember any part of my life, after being settled in it, that I have not constantly been in the same sentiment, always looking beyond the bounds of time and desiring to quit the gift for the Giver."[17] It was just that, like anything good and desirable, it took practice to acquire in all its purity.

It is not surprising that, in those earlier days of her life, "after being settled in it", her attraction to eternity itself, with her from infancy, should still at times take bumbling expression. It could, for instance, be cavalier, as when she told Julia: "I am jogging on old style, trying to accomplish every duty, and *hoping* for the reward; without that in view, heaven knows this life would be a scene of confusion and vexation *to me,* who neither values it nor desires it. I always thought, and ever shall, *that husbands can be consoled,* children sometimes prosper as well without as with parents; and, at all events, life has such varieties of disappointments that they may as well proceed from one cause as another."[18] The best that can be said for such high-handed sentiments is that they are amazing. Elizabeth must have been feeling a bit giddy and feckless the day she wrote them. That she, sober and earnest to the nth degree, was truly serious can be immediately rejected.

Her enthusiasm could be clumsy, as when she wished her friend Eliza Sadler "Happy Birthday" by sending her some prayers of preparation for death! Mrs. Sadler was predictably upset, and Elizabeth wrote in apology: "My own Eliza, I fear you did not understand sufficiently my meaning in the use of those little prayers I gave you—which was to impress on your mind the necessity of preparing for a blessed death. . . . I have observed, dear, that any good resolutions or exercises begun on the period of our birth are more seriously impressed, and chose this for you at this time, as reflecting on a birthday on earth more easily transfers our thoughts to the birthday of our future existence."[19]

Elizabeth could be just a bit priggish, even unwittingly cruel, as witness her answer to a bewildered Julia, who had long had no letters from her: "How many reproaches my heart makes me when I think of you. So many years I have called you dear friend, and shall your dear friend be insincere to you? Dear Julia, then I will tell you the plain truth, that my habits both of soul and body are changed, that I feel all the habits of society and connections of *this* life have taken a new form, and are only interesting or endearing as they point the view to the next."[20]

Both of these letters demonstrate the very human reaction to discovery of something new and enchanting. Having glimpsed the inviting depths of the spiritual life, Elizabeth had, like a child with a new toy, to show them off to others who had no comprehension of them. Yet awkward as these yearnings for eternity were, they were nonetheless true and deeply felt, the very reason that her love for husband and children grew ever more solicitous, that Eliza was pacified, that Julia and Elizabeth corresponded faithfully until the latter's death.

Elizabeth was always a quick learner, and in her *Leghorn Journal,* written in the year after her unconscious rebuff to Julia, there emerges for the first time *eternity* not only as the never-ending love of God but also as the reunion with loved ones—the first faint glimmer of the fruitful and constant communion of saints. Far from home or any knowledge of it, nursing a dying husband in the dank quarantine horror of Livorno's (Leghorn's) *lazaretto,* she wrote: "Dear home, dearest sisters, my little ones—well—either protected by God in this world or in heaven. It is a sweet thought to dwell on, that all those I most tenderly love, *love God;* and if we do not meet again *here, there* we shall be separated *no more.* If I have lost them *now,* their gain is infinite and eternal."[21]

The doctrine of the communion of saints has not only the general and objective aspects of interaction among God's people in heaven, in purgatory and on earth but also the intimate union of family and friends, living and deceased, at any desired moment of prayer. All are ever one, ever near, in the realm of the spirit. It was only a matter of time before Elizabeth's heart for family and friends should discover so satisfying a reality. In the *lazaretto* she had not unfolded it completely, dwelling only on future reunion, not yet fully aware of the communion of the living, except for God's mutual protection.

Years later, when Elizabeth had indeed lost her firstborn, Anna Maria, who had been with her throughout that ordeal in the *lazaretto,* the calm truths she had adverted to and invoked there were useless to prevent deep, deep anguish of soul and body. She was literally torn apart. As she told a friend, "For three months after Nina was taken I was so often expecting to lose my senses, and my head was so disordered, that unless for the daily duties always before me, I did not know much what I did or what I left undone."[22]

The fact of eternity had its part in purifying the souls of mother and child for the reunion it promised. "Poor, poor Mother, let her talk to you, Eliza", Elizabeth cried out to Mrs. Sadler when the floodgates of her grief had broken.

> If you could have seen at the moment when kneeling at the foot of her bed to rub her cold, cold feet a day or two before [her death]—she saw the tears, and without being able to hide her own, tho' smiling at the same time, she repeated the so-often asked question: "Can it be for me? Should you not rejoice? It will be but a moment, and reunited for Eternity. A happy eternity with my Mother—what a thought!" These were her very words. And when in death's agony her quivering lips could with difficulty utter one word, feeling a tear fall on her face, she smiled, and said with great effort: "Laugh, Mother, Jesus!"— at intervals, as she could not put two words together. Poor Mother must say no more; only pray, Eliza, that she may be strengthened. . . . You believe me when I say with my whole soul, "His Will be done forever!" Eternity was Anna's darling word. I find it written in everything that belonged to her: music, books, copies, the walls of her little chamber, everywhere that word.[23]

Who had taught her that word?

In the teaching, Elizabeth herself had learned the hard lesson that eternal reunion with loved ones is often only won by separation from them here. That sting was in a letter to Julia Scott, nearly a year later: "I sit writing by the window, opposite my darling darling's *little Wood*. The white palings appear thro' the trees. Oh, Julia, my Julia, if we may but pass our dear eternity together! Are you good? Do you try to be good? I try with my whole heart. I long so to get above this blue horizon. Oh, my Anna, the child of my soul! All, all my dear ones so many years gone before! ETERNAL REUNION!"[24]

How well Elizabeth had learned the lesson is evident in contrasting even her human reaction to the death of her youngest, Rebecca, four years later: "The Mother is a miracle of divine favor", noted Father John Dubois, Superior of the Sisterhood. "Night and day by the child, her health has not appeared to suffer. She held the child in her arms without dropping a tear, all the time of her agony and even eight minutes after she had died. *Mulierem fortem.* "[25] When she herself slipped sharply toward eternity, two years after Bec, she wrote joyfully to a friend: "Bec's birthday. She would be 16, but counts time no more, sweet darling—what a thought to go to *her* and our *Nina,* to go to *God.* "[26]

The sacrifice of separation to win everlasting reunion had already taken firm root in Elizabeth's soul with her son William's departure for Italy to train for commerce with the Filicchis in 1815. She would see very little of him in the remaining five years of her life. On his eighteenth birthday, a month before he left, she first sounded the theme she would worry until the day she died: letting go of him here to be with him forever. "You know your *Mother's heart*", she wrote in her birthday note. "It had a dear communication for you, for *our eternity,* my William. Be blessed a thousand, thousand times! Take a few little moments in the church today, in union with your Mother's heart, to place yourself again and again in the hands of God. Do, my dearest one."[27] She had not abandoned her strategy of using earthly birthdays as reminders of heavenly ones; she had only refined it.

Elizabeth's reminders to William became a gradual crescendo in ensuing years, gathering in intensity as her fears increased. The intensity and the fears had their source in Elizabeth's predilection for her firstborn son. She owned it quite frankly. She wrote him in unusually intimate vein as he awaited naval assignment in Boston in 1818: "Last night I had you close where you used to lie so snug and warm when you drew the *life stream* twenty years ago, and where the heart still beats to love you dearly, dearly till its last sigh, *which even then* loved you *best of all.* "[28] And again: "I often ask, but what is this dear rover to me so much more than all the world? Why do the heart strings all wind round him so? *That I cannot tell.* Let it pass, for it depends not on me."[29]

Elizabeth confided this primacy of love and her bewilderment over it to Antonio Filicchi in a letter that at the same time absolved her of all foolish maternal bias: "I cannot hide from Our God, though from everyone else I must conceal, the perpetual tears and affections of boundless gratitude which overflow my heart when I think of him secure in his *Faith* and your protection. Why I love him so much I cannot account, but own to you, Antonio, all my weakness. Pity and pray for a mother attached to her children through such peculiar motives as I am to mine. I purify it as much as I can, and Our Lord knows it is their souls alone I look at."[30] She confirmed the purity of her maternal love in her very last letter to Antonio: "For many years I have had no prayer for my children but that Our Blessed God would do everything to them and in them in the way of affliction and adversity, if only—He will save their soul(s)!"[31]

In light of future events—William seems indeed to have faltered for a time in the practice of his faith—Elizabeth's partiality may well have been, all unknown to her, the partiality of the Good Shepherd for the strayed and lost of His flock. In any event, there can be no discounting the anguish of her separation from her older son or the terror with which she urged her own "dear eternity" upon him, with a mother's love as her means of persuasion.

"Be sure, as I told you, to remain faithful to your external duties", was Elizabeth's welcome to William on his arrival at the Filicchis in Livorno. "Write me how often you have been to the sacred tribunal since you left me. Child of my soul, *be good* and *be happy!* The only thought that frightens me when I feel weak and faint is that I will see you no more in this world. But that is nothing, *if only in the next....* O my William, tears will overpower— and my soul cries to our eternity. My dear, dear one, if the world should draw you from Our God, and we not meet there! That thought I cannot stand."[32] When William's restless nature showed signs of dissatisfaction with the world of trade, Elizabeth's foreboding that he might leave the spiritual haven of her pious friends—

which he had indeed already resolved to do—prompted her to write in panic:

> My soul's own William: The bitter, freezing North wind is now always rattling, and they write me on every side—New York and Baltimore—that the ice will let no vessel go to you. Yet, my head and heart is so full of you, that though letters for you are waiting at both ports, I must write. If I wake in the night, I think it is your angel wakes me to pray for you. And last night I found myself actually dropping asleep, repeating your name over and over, and appealing to Our Lord with the agony of a mother's love for our long and dear and everlasting reunion.[33]

That agony reached an almost unbearable peak as she lay dying:

> William, William, William, is it possible the cry of my heart doesn't reach yours? I carry your beloved name before the tabernacle and repeat it there as my prayers in torrents of tears which Our Lord alone understands. Childish weakness, fond partiality, you would say half-pained, if you could see from *your present scene* the agonized heart of your Mother. But its agony is not for our present separation, my beloved one; it is on long, eternal years, which press on it beyond all expression. To love you here a few years of so embittered a life is but the common lot; but to love as I love you, and lose you forever—oh, unutterable anguish! A whole eternity miserable, a whole eternity the enemy of God, and such a God as He is to us—!

The wild outburst of pain, which she no longer cared to conceal, ended almost despairing: "Reading so much, your faith is quite lost, having everything to extinguish and nothing to nourish it. My William, William, William, if I did not see your doting Bec and Nina above, what would save my heart from breaking?"[34]

This maternal pain, constant over the years and never assuaged, should be seen against the daily round of Elizabeth's religious life. The heartache she shared with all mothers was not visited on her Sisters; she let no part of its burden fall on them. She led the prayers, presided over meals and recreation and directed the school-work like any other superior and principal. Only in the night, when all were in bed and the house still and her physical pain and hacking cough would not let her sleep, would she "draw up the little basket of chips you so well remember", she told William, "make up a small blaze in your stove",[35] and in so many nights put on paper the fear that haunted her soul. For one so holy the fear and consequent pain of the sword in the heart must have been truly exquisite.

No saint ever had a more constant eye on eternity than Elizabeth Seton. It was the star she steered by. It motivated everything—love of God and neighbor, every action spiritual and temporal. It was the refrain of her teaching, the silent watchdog of her conscience. It was the spur to every good action, the barrier to every omission.

"Eternity, oh how near it often seems to me. Think of it when you are hard pushed", Elizabeth urged a friend, bowed under trials. "How long will be that day without a night or that night without a day. May we praise and bless and adore forever."[36] There was an essential rightness, therefore, in "her dear eternity's" being the Amen to her sojourn on earth. When, in the small hours of New Year's Day 1821, the Sister nursing her came with the scheduled medicine, the saint pushed it aside. "Never mind the drink", she said. "One Communion more—and then eternity."[37]

Father Simon Gabriel Bruté.

3

"HIS BLESSED WILL"

While saints are one in their heroicity of holiness, each has a hallmark, some distinguishing quality of virtue or apostolate. With Francis of Assisi, it is his love of poverty; with Francis de Sales, his gentleness and affability; with Thérèse of Lisieux, her simple "little way" of loving God; with Vincent de Paul, his devotion to the poor.

The hallmark of St. Elizabeth Ann Seton is her love of the Will of God—not only her *submission* to that holy Will but also her *love* of it. She defined it simply and uncompromisingly as early as 1804: "God has given me a great deal to do", she confided to Julia Scott, "and I have always and hope always to prefer His Will to every wish of my own."[1] Her choice of the word *prefer* is a sure indication of committed love.

Even to submit to God's Will demands faith, but when faith is nourished to the point of taking over one's whole existence and governing one's every act, mere submission is transformed to an eager acceptance that can only be born of love. St. Elizabeth Ann quickly progressed even beyond such acceptance to a *reaching out* for what God offered.

Faith and love then become so intertwined that they can scarcely be distinguished, and it may be asked why they should be. Even on a purely human plane, trust must be at the root of all true love. Elizabeth Seton expressed it with shining clarity: "Faith lifts the staggering soul on one side, Hope supports it on the other. Experi-

ence says it must be, and love says—let it be."[2] Let it be. Without
these words, all is a submission; with them, all is love—not a
grudging "well, if I have to" but a glad, wholehearted "yes".
Elizabeth's practical perception, "Experience says it must be"—
nothing can really be done about most of life's happenings—echoes
Jesus' injunction to Saul on the road to Damascus, "It is hard for
you, kicking like this against the goad", but "Let it be" is also an
echo, the sublime echo of Saul's humble answer, "What am I to
do, Lord?"[3]

Elizabeth's faith was the faith of Abraham, who left his own
country at God's word, who believed on the same word that his
aging and barren wife would conceive and bear the father of
a numberless people, yet who was willing to sacrifice his son of
the promise at the same word. Elizabeth's love was the love of Job,
who cried to the Lord, "Even if you should kill me, still would
I love you"; of the Vincentian martyr John Gabriel Perboyre,
who, in a dark night of the soul during his passion, became
convinced that he would be damned, yet begged the Lord, "If
I cannot love You in the next world, at least let me love You in
this one." Elizabeth gave tongue to this same fathomless faith, this
same limitless love, as her last, long decline began: "Oh, if all goes
well for me what will I not do for you!" she promised her
director, Father Simon Gabriel Bruté. "You will see. But, alas, yet
if I am not one of His elect, it is only I to be blamed, and when
going down I must still lift the hands to the very last look in praise
and gratitude for what He has done to save me. What more could
He have done? That thought stops all."[4]

Elizabeth early sealed her love in the Lord's own way with a
covenant. At twenty-eight she was a deeply pious Episcopalian,
but until that time her piety had been eclectic and random for
want of someone to put it in order. However, Henry Hobart, the
young curate of Trinity Church, had recently come into her life
and taken charge of her soul. What before she had only sensed she
now comprehended. As sure knowledge grew in the structure of
an ordered spirituality, she made the indispensable and irrevocable
choice, setting it down thus:

This blessed day, Sunday, 23rd May 1802, my soul was first sensibly conceived of the blessing and practicability of an entire surrender of itself and all its faculties to God. It has been the *Lord's Day* indeed to me, though many, many temptations to forget my heavenly possession *in His constant Presence* have pressed upon me. But—blessed be my gracious Shepherd!—in this last hour of *His Day* I am at rest within His fold, sweetly refreshed with the waters of comfort which have flowed through the soul of his ministering servant, our blessed teacher [Hobart]. Glory to my God for this unspeakable blessing! Glory to my God for the means of grace and the hopes of glory which He so mercifully bestows on his unworthy servant! O Lord, before Thee I must ever be unworthy until covered with the robe of righteousness by my beloved Redeemer. He shall fit me to behold the vision of Thy glory.[5]

The language is lushly biblical, even pompous. Indeed, Elizabeth's addiction to such "Protestant expressions" embarrassed her in later years. At the time, however, it was the only spiritual language she knew, and there can be no mistaking the sincerity of her feeling and devotion.

Father Bruté has characterized faith as "Mother's eminent disposition"—"FAITH"—he wrote the word in large letters—"and whole trust in God for herself, [her] children", the "only desire, *Salvation*".[6] He then went on to prove the rightness of his judgment by quoting Elizabeth's own words: "One thing I have asked of the Lord, one thing only, and will persist in asking, and will hang upon Him for, and for which I think I have his promise, ever the life of their and my soul."[7] The words are simple and scriptural, the faith simple, too, but, oh, how immense and unyielding! In another place, Bruté has categorized Elizabeth's faith in those things she especially loved, "the Church, the Blessed Sacrament, prayer for herself and her children, the Blessed Virgin, and the priestly character".[8]

In Elizabeth's *Dear Remembrances,* she records her emotions in preparing for the voyage to Italy with her dying husband, and the emotions are wholly prophetic: "At 29—Faith in our Leghorn voyage, reliance that *all* would turn to good"[9]—she was not so naïve as to think that Will could recover, but she spoke of the greater ambit of the future, her own and her children's, and yes, hidden from her then, her country's and the world's—"delight in packing up all our valuables to be sold, the adieu to each article to be mine no more"[10]—then the strangest and most specifically prophetic of all—"thousand secret hopes in God of separation from the world".[11]

When Elizabeth had put her covenant in writing, she felt immediately the reward of surrendering all, the heavenly peace not of the world: "My peace I leave with you, my peace I give unto you, not as the world gives give I unto you—let not your hearts be troubled, neither be afraid"—she savored the sweetness of the words of giving and promise—"This gift from Our blessed Lord is the testimony of His love, the earnest of His continued affection, and the perfection of future blessedness to His faithful and obedient servants, *which* is the consummation of this Peace in the vision of celestial presence and glory. From Him it proceeds, to Him it tends, and in Him concentrates."[12] She understood so well that Christ was all, and everything in Him. The understanding enlightened and directed her prayer, as we shall see, making it forthright and fruitful.

Four months later—"Sunday, 12th September, three weeks and two days after the birth of *my Rebecca,* I renewed my covenant that I would strive with myself and use every earnest endeavor to serve my dear Redeemer and to give myself wholly unto Him."[13] The lengthening weeks of perseverance and quiet determination are unwavering proof that Elizabeth's total giving of herself was no passing whim or fancy. The next day's entry in her *Journal* was of even more importance, for it actualized what she had promised: "Began a new life—resumed the occupations and duties which fill up the part He has assigned me."[14] How well she understood, even then, that perfection was not pursued in high-flown phrases but by fidelity to the duties and drudgeries of everyday life. How well she grasped the mystical truth that, while the "occupations and duties" were the same, she had indeed begun a new life because her covenant had transformed them and "made all things new". A short time later the Great Act was completed, when Elizabeth seized upon the occasion of preparing the bedside table of a dying parishioner of Trinity for the reception of Communion to hail the Sacrament as "the seal of that Covenant which I trust will not be broken in life nor in death, in time nor in eternity"— a true, anticipated Catholic perception of the Eucharist as "the pledge of future glory".[15]

Elizabeth Seton had entered into her covenant, which was to rule the rest of her life, with eyes wide open. She knew from bitter experience what it would demand of her. Behind her was the loneliness of a neglected childhood spent as an uncertain guest of relatives (her father was immersed in medicine; her stepmother had children of her own). Elizabeth's married life, though happy, had had its fill of loved ones' illnesses and deaths. Even as she wrote the precious agreement with her Lord, she was living in greatly reduced circumstances because of the failure of her husband's business, and he himself was far gone in tuberculosis. She was soon to suffer even more acutely through his last illness and death in the dank horror of Livorno's *lazaretto,* or quarantine, and the subsequent long, drawn-out anguish of her own conversion to the Catholic Faith. Her conversion would bring fresh trials in the ostracism of family and friends and her frustrated efforts to earn bread for her children.[16]

None of these moved Elizabeth from her committed path. "Renewed the *entire* sacrifice fervently", she wrote in her *Journal* in the summer of 1807. "Yielded all and offered every nerve, fibre and power of soul and body to sickness, death at any and every appointment of His Blessed Will."[17] And she assured Antonio Filicchi:

I repeat to you, Antonio (as you may be anxious on the subject), these are my happiest days. Sometimes the harassed mind, wearied with continual contradiction to all it would most covet—solitude! silence! peace!—sighs for a change; but five minutes' recollection procures an immediate act of resignation, convinced

that this is the day of salvation for me. And if, like a coward,
I should run away from the field of battle, I am sure the very
peace I seek would fly from me, and the state of penance
sanctified by the Will of God would be again wished for as the
safest and surest road.[18]

Elizabeth had indeed learned the hard way how to love God, to
do what *He* wanted, not what *she* wanted, however good and
holy it seemed, and to wait for Him to reveal what He wanted by
circumstances. Thus far, circumstances of persons, illness, death
and revelation had changed her life radically at every turning.
A wife at twenty, she was a widow at twenty-nine. She had
chosen the married state but was led inexorably to the religious
life. She had lived fervently in the Episcopal Communion as few
before or since yet was harried by grace to a Church despised by
all the world she knew, a circumstance that finally drove her from
her beloved native place.

Yet the pain of exile forced from her only an affirmation of the
divine Will she had come to love with her whole being. "I saw
once more the windows of State Street," she wrote of the parting
to Eliza Sadler,

> passed the Quarantine, and so near the shore as to see every part
> of it. Oh, my Lord—in that hour! Can a heart swell so high and
> not burst? . . . My Eliza, think of me, when you pass it again,
> battering the waves of my changeable life. Yet would I change one
> shade or trial of it—that would be madness, and working in the
> dark. Oh, no—the dear, dear, dear adored Will be done through
> every moment of it! And may it control, regulate and perfect us;
> and when all is over, how we will rejoice that it was done![19]

The affirmation was repeated as she sat writing far into the night
on board the *Grand Sachem* in Baltimore Harbor, June 15, 1808,
waiting to land the next day: "Tomorrow, do I go among strangers?"
she asked in her *Journal.* "No. Has an anxious thought or fear
passed my mind? No. Can I be disappointed? No. One sweet
Sacrifice will reunite my soul with all who offer it. Doubt and
fear fly from the breast inhabited by *Him.* There can be no

disappointment where the soul's only desire and expectation is to meet His Adored Will and fulfill it."[20]

Here was a total commitment to an unknown future, a serene commitment, gladly accepting whatever trials that future might hold. And this deeply personal commitment is wrapped with theological surety in the Mystical Body of Christ and its common offering of the holy Sacrifice of the Mass. From hindsight it can be stated that the loving docility that had brought Elizabeth Ann Seton, against all odds, to Baltimore, and its fruition in Emmitsburg, was one of God's great gifts to the Church in America.

The haven of Catholic Baltimore and the security of support for her children in the little school provided there might have led a soul less seasoned than Elizabeth to look for a halt in the roll of events or circumstances and their contrarieties. She knew better. She was satisfied that her own good was "always best advanced in poverty and in tears".[21]

There is little doubt that linked with Elizabeth's germinating apostolate of Catholic education planted in Baltimore was the culmination of a desire for the religious life. It was hinted at in a letter to Antonio Filicchi in 1805: "I have a little secret to communicate to you when we meet (a sweet dream of imagination)";[22] and in another, the following year: "If you were here now, my dear brother, I think you would exert your friendship for us and obtain the so long desired refuge of a place in the Order of St. Francis for your converts."[23] At Baltimore the desire flowered into reality as "my, or rather the scheme of these revered gentlemen (the Sulpician Fathers)".[24] Less than a month after her arrival Elizabeth told Antonio Filicchi, "It is proposed to . . . begin on a small plan admitting of enlargement if necessary, in the hope and expectation that there will not be wanting ladies to join in forming a permanent institution."[25] Three months later she was calling herself "your poor little Nun" in a letter to Julia Scott and assuring Cecilia Seton, "It is expected I shall be the Mother of many daughters."[26]

An unforeseen obstacle reared momentarily amid this euphoria when Elizabeth was introduced to Samuel Sutherland Cooper, a wealthy Philadelphia convert who was about to enter St. Mary's Seminary. They were attracted to each other—and marriage would have solved handsomely the problem of support for Elizabeth's children. She admitted quite candidly to Cecilia Seton that "if we had not devoted ourselves to the heavenly spouse before we met, I do not know how the attraction would have terminated";[27] but, she assured Julia Scott, "the only result of this partiality has been the encouragement of each other to persevere in the path which each has chosen".[28] The seeming obstacle was in reality an integral part of the unfolding of God's Will, for Cooper was to be the necessary benefactor of the proposed Sisterhood and school.

It is important to note that, despite Elizabeth's passing and quickly corrected "my", the proposal and its development were wholly the works of the Sulpician Fathers. She wanted it that way in her usual waiting on God's Will and fearing to force it. Her only wish, far from being a foundress, was to live in religion and make herself "useful as an assistant in teaching".[29] Her only activity in the matter was to attempt to interest the Filicchis in supporting the plan financially, for it seemed natural to her to look for God's Will in that direction while at the same time leaving things wide open to Him. "In every daily Mass and at Communion, I beg Him to prepare your heart, and our dear Antonio's, to dispose of me and mine in any way which may please Him", she told Filippo Filicchi. "You are our Father in Him; through your hands we received the new and precious being which is indeed true life." But Elizabeth's basic stance was plain: "All is in His hands. If I had a choice, and my will would decide in a moment, I would remain silent in His hands. Oh, how sweet it is, there to rest in perfect confidence."[30] And again, the humble and wise recognition of what was good for her: "For my part, I shall naturally look for disappointments, and have always found them so conducive to the soul's advancement, that if we succeed in forming the proposed establishment I shall look upon it as a sure mark that Almighty God intends an extensive benefit without calculating my particular interest, which is always best advanced in poverty and in tears."[31]

Of course, Elizabeth was right to expect disappointments, to expect her directors' plans to be contradicted. Experience had taught her so, and so it was.

The Sisters were to staff "an institution for the advancement of Catholic female children in habits of religion".[32] Specifically, Elizabeth later told Antonio Filicchi, it was Cooper's "meaning and my hopes" that it "was to have been a nursery only for Our Savior's poor country children", but, she admitted, "it seems it is to be the forming of city girls to faith and piety as wives and mothers".[33] And these city girls were from comfortable families who could afford to pay for their schooling—they had formed the nucleus of the Baltimore school, and it soon became evident that no establishment could succeed without regular income.

Besides, she told Filippo Filicchi, Mr. Cooper "desires extremely to extend the plan to the reception of the aged, and also uneducated persons, who may be employed in spinning, knitting, etc., so as to found a manufactory on a small scale which may be beneficial to the poor".[34] The "manufactory" was never heard of again.

The establishment was to be in Baltimore. It was made at Emmitsburg, "contrary to all the former convictions of this ecclesiastic [Dubourg] and those of the founders"—according to Dubourg himself—"and what is still more astonishing, in spite of the strongest opposition of the venerable Archbishop Carroll, who yielded at last to the force of circumstances."[35]

Circumstances and contradictions again—and they were not to cease.

The Sisterhood an established fact, Elizabeth's first and lasting contradiction was intensely personal. She simply did not like being a religious superior, a distaste with which many religious superiors can surely empathize. Certainly her heart was high at the realization of her "sweet dream of imagination" and the life of charity it offered, when she wrote to Julia Scott two days before pronouncing private vows of poverty, chastity and obedience: "To speak the joy of my soul at the prospect of being able to assist the poor, visit the sick, comfort the sorrowful, clothe little innocents and teach them to love God!—there I must stop!"[36] But some time later, when she and the first little band of recruits were discussing the future of the community with Archbishop Carroll and some of his priests, the full force of what she had undertaken bore down suddenly on her soul. She cried uncontrollably for some minutes; then, falling to her knees, she confessed before them all her faults and sins committed since childhood and, with arms raised to heaven, sobbed out: "My gracious God! You know my unfitness for this task. I, who by my sins have so often crucified You, I blush with shame and confusion. How can I teach others, who know so little myself, and am so miserable and imperfect?"[37]

This conviction of unworthiness never left Elizabeth. When the Rule was formally ratified in 1812, Mother Seton wrote in her *Journal*: "Eternity! Mother! What a celestial commission entrusted! Mother of the Daughters of Charity, by whom so much is to do also for God through their short life!"[38]

In a strictly human sense, Elizabeth was quite right about her unworthiness to be not only a superior but also a foundress. A convert of only four years, she knew as little as her artless Sisters about the religious life. When she and they entered retreat at Emmitsburg on August 10, 1809, it was the first retreat any of them had made. It was to be expected, therefore, that this further solemn step in the community's development—when she dwelt upon its fresh call to duty and candidly recognized her own lack of experience—should reawaken the uneasiness of her soul.

Sister Cecilia O'Conway, Elizabeth's first recruit, countered it with fond, wise advice: "My beloved Mother, how [you] surprise me by your *alarm* on the duties of a Superior", the girl wrote.

Precious soul, what is the difference between it and those of a *Christian parent?* . . . Spiritual parent[s] must be both attentive to soul and body, attentive to keep the proud and self-willed under *obedience,* the same restrained as a spoiled child, yielding with parental indulgence where neither sin, fault nor breach of rules are in danger. . . . Be a mild, patient *but firm* MAMMA, and you need not tremble under the burden of superiority. Jesus can never give you a task above your courage, strength or ability.

Come, precious darling, don't let uneasiness and fear appear so plain to the weak. You must at least be the MOON, if the sun is too bright and too dignified a character. The more gentle and modest light will suit our valley in the growing fervor of your little Company.

Gratefully, Elizabeth wrote on the back of the letter: "Cecilia's admirable lesson to me."[39]

Father Gabriel Bruté, Elizabeth's spiritual director and dear friend, has attested to the pain religious motherhood caused her, that she was "little inclined [to] preach to others . . . to have as a Superior to instruct, direct, reprove . . . so impressed that she did poorly, badly, neglectfully, and to the injury of souls."[40] This was a cross, indeed, to be obliged to "instruct, direct, reprove" her Sisters and at the same time to be convinced that she was actually harming their good and trusting souls! Elizabeth herself described her pain humbly but graphically: "Conscience reproaches aloud— how little charity and delicacy of love I practice in that vile habit of speaking of the faults of others", she confessed to Bruté, "of the *short, cold, repulsive conduct* to my betters, as all certainly are, and for much of my behavior to you, my visible savior, I would put it out (especially some words of reproach and disappointment the other day) I would put them out with my blood! I am in one continual watch to keep down my eyebrows and wear the ready smile, if even it sometimes be 'ghastly!' "[41]

Basically, Elizabeth had the saint's honest distrust of self. All her tasks as superior were not harsh and displeasing, but the pleasant ones she distrusted most of all, as she confessed to Bruté, "This part of *sitting at the pen smiling at the people* young and old, it is too dangerously pleasing"—yet even here—"His dear Will in all, though".[42] Like all saints, she had microscopic sight of her soul's imperfections and a purity of love that made them an agony to her. Ordinary men are inclined to smile at the saints' apprehensions of guilt as exaggerations. They are nothing of the kind. Saints understand the full horror of sin. The smallest imperfection stands out black and stark against the whiteness of their souls. Vincent de

Paul demonstrated this clear-eyed vision when, admonishing a brother for calling him "a marvel", replied that he was indeed a marvel, but a marvel of malice, more wicked than the devil, who had less reason to be in hell than he; and the saint added that he did not exaggerate.[43]

Bruté understood the supreme standards of the saints and, therefore, even during the last retreat of Elizabeth's life, did not hesitate to admonish her "to keep a good exterior and to flee from harsh words; and in exercising authority to have a certain modesty and goodness, because this will inspire confidence and love", and prodded her sense of accountability by reminding her that "God gives you this . . . naturally".[44] Yet his judgment of the minuteness of guilt in Elizabeth is evident in her honest acknowledgment: "As to *private* concerns, I have none, unless it be my trials occasionally at the conduct of different Sisters, and that you have forbid me speaking of; and since you think proper, and I am acquitted before God, I am too happy it is so."[45] Bruté made his judgment public after Elizabeth's death: she was, he attested, "a true pattern to her Sisters: their mother for love, their servant for humility, their true superior for prudent guidance, their friend in every pain they felt".[46]

Striking examples that Elizabeth was indeed "their friend in every pain" were her vigorous defenses of the Sisters' rights. The first occurred at the very outset of their community life. For reasons best known to himself, Father William Dubourg, their first superior, forbade them to go to confession to his confrere Father Pierre Babade, whom the Sisters considered their first spiritual father, and to cease all correspondence with him. The second was even more serious for the community's durability. Father John Baptist David, who despite Mother Seton's expressed misgivings had been appointed second superior of the Sisterhood when Dubourg had resigned in a huff over the Babade affair and Elizabeth's forthright reaction to it, took over the community as his private fief, usurped the Mother's office and even determined to replace her with his protégé, Sister Rose White. His actions came close to destroying the company before it was firmly established.

Both these crises, by exacerbating Elizabeth's innate distaste for ruling, were serious tests of her commitment to God's Will and her religious obedience. She was candid about the anguish they caused her and intrepid in suffering it. "I have had a great many hard trials, my Father, since you were here", she confessed to Archbishop Carroll,

> but you, of course, will congratulate me on them, as the fire of tribulation is no doubt meant to consume the many imperfections and bad dispositions Our Lord finds in me. Indeed, it has at times burnt so deep that the anguish could not be concealed; but by degrees custom reconciles pain itself, and I determine, dry and hard as my daily bread is, to take it with as good grace as possible. When I carry it before Our Lord, sometimes He makes me laugh at myself and asks me what other kind I would choose in the valley of tears than that which Himself and all His followers made use of.[47]

And to her friend Matthias O'Conway she made a truly startling admission: "You will laugh at me when I tell you I have seen more real affliction and sorrow here in the ten months since our removal [from Baltimore] than in all the thirty-five years of my past life, which was all marked by affliction", she wrote. "You will laugh, I repeat, because you will know that the fruit will not be lost — or, at least, I hope not; though, indeed, sometimes I tremble."[48] The deaths of Harriet and Cecilia Seton and the constant illness in the house were, to be sure, part of the affliction and sorrow, but it cannot be doubted that the assaults on the peace and future of her community were uppermost.

Elizabeth continued to do what she had to do, much as she disliked it, because "the Dearest says, 'You shall, you must, only because I will it.' "[49] She believed that He spoke to her through her Archbishop, who wrote of her community and her office, "It is not to flatter or nourish pride . . . that I declare an opinion and belief that its ultimate success under God depends on your sacrificing yourself, notwithstanding all the uneasiness and disgust you may experience, and continuing in your place of superior."[50] And again: "If you should ever be permitted to resign your maternal charge over your community, I would rejoice on your own individual account, but my hope for the continuance of the establishment would be very much weakened."[51] It was not the first time Elizabeth waited for the revelation of the Will of God on the nod of a superior, no matter for how long, or the first time she waited for Carroll's approval. When Cecilia Seton was detained in New York at the insistence of her pastor, Elizabeth had laid the matter before Carroll. "Whatever he decides," she told Cecilia, "I will conclude to be the Will of God, and will never say one word more about your joining me until it pleases him to show us it is right."[52]

Elizabeth was not yet a spiritual adept, but her heart was right—lowly and obedient. When Dubourg, to her dismay, had resigned—an action she had never intended or wanted—she admitted humbly to Carroll: "In my place, my dear Father, you would have experienced my trial, but you would at once have offered it up to God. I am late in seeing the necessity of this measure, but not too late, I hope, since it is never too late with Our good Lord. . . . You will see how good a child I am going to be. Quite a little child. And perhaps you will have to give me the food of little children yet, but I will do my best as I have promised you in every case."[53]

It would never be too late for Elizabeth Seton for, however she might stumble, her eyes were fixed on God and her "dear eternity", and she knew and accepted the rough road ahead. "His Adorable Will be done during the few remaining days of my tiresome journey," she wrote with finality to her friend George Weis, "which, being made with so many tears and sown so thick with crosses, will certainly be concluded with joy and crowned with eternal rest".[54]

How many testimonies there are to Elizabeth's clear-sighted—and farsighted—vision and hard-won acceptance! When the Archbishop and Elizabeth's "Reverend Gentlemen" were pondering the feasibility of having a mother with five children as the head of a religious community, she stated her own position simply to

Weis: "Here I stand with hands and eyes both lifted to wait the Adorable Will. The only word I have to say to every question is: *I am a mother.* Whatever providence awaits me consistent with that plea, I say Amen to it."[55] Indeed, she reminded the Archbishop that "surely, an individual is not to be considered where a public good is in question; and you know I would gladly make every sacrifice you think consistent with my first and inseparable obligations as a mother."[56] It was on the occasion of one or another of the succession of decisions made by her superiors, decisions that affected her deeply, that she wrote calmly: "At this very time the question must be in motion, and the Adored's vote will decide." Such a surety that God would always prevail made life tranquil underneath the storms of contradictions and pain.

God did not wait for eternity to reward Elizabeth's steadfastness. When the long, drawn-out turmoil of clerical interference was ended with Carroll's first approval of the Rule, he assured her that the future would free her "from a state in which it was difficult to walk straight, as you had no certain way in which to proceed".[57] Nothing like the Babade controversy would ever again be allowed to disturb peace of soul, for "every allowance shall be made not only to the Sisters generally, but to each one in particular".[58] As for usurpation of authority, like David's, not only would no Sulpician "but your immediate superior, residing near you . . . have any share in the government or concerns of the Sisters",[59] but also even his role was generally to be restricted. The Archbishop made plain his will "to confine the administrations of your own affairs, and the internal and domestic government, as much as possible, to your own institutions once adopted, and within your own walls. Your Superior or confessor need be informed or consulted in matters where the Mother and her Council need his advice."[60] The wisdom of the Father of the Church in America never shone more brightly than in these determinations.

The peace and reward that had come to her community did not, of course, exempt Elizabeth from the personal testing that she had long recognized as "the safest and surest" way to sanctity and heaven. When Annina was torn from Elizabeth, she freely confessed the depths of her grief: "The separation from my angel has left so new and deep an impression on my mind, that if I was not obliged to live in these dear ones, I should unconsciously die in her"—but, lest she be misunderstood—"unconsciously," she repeated, "for never by a free act of the mind will I ever regret *His Will*".[61] The separation from her youngest, Rebecca, was still to be endured as well as the separations in this world from her restless sons, to say nothing of the constant heartbreaks from their thoughtlessness and her terror for their souls. Her unswerving attitude of soul in it all would ever be, nonetheless, an echo of her cry to Julia Scott in the midst of the sickness and death of that first horrible Christmas at Emmitsburg: "Here I go like iron or rock, day after day, *as He pleases and how He pleases;* but, to be sure, when my turn comes I shall be very glad."[62] Even the unending string of personal trials were, however, softened with extraordinary graces, of which the gift of Gabriel Bruté as spiritual director and friend was the chief. Rejoicing in his understanding of her eager, bursting soul, Elizabeth exulted: "Blessed G., I am so in love now with rules that I see the *bit* of the bridle all gold, or the *reins* all of silk. You know my sincerity, since, with the little attraction to your Brother's [Dubois'] government, I even eagerly seek the grace [of the] little cords he entangles me with."[63]

Elizabeth's greatest reward was the divine, contemplative peace of her last months. "I once told you how I wished to do as you have done," she finished a letter of advice to a priest friend, "and I will tell you *in return,* that all the illusion and spider web of *earthly weaving* is broken, and nothing more bright and steady than the *divine lamp* He feeds and trims Himself, because, as I suppose, I stayed in *obedience.* Oh, this *Master and Father!* . . . How can we be happy enough in His service?"[64] She did not mean obedience to any particular hierarchical supervisor, priest or director but to the Will of God she had loved with her whole soul and which she had sought *through* her superiors and in the events and contradictions of a constantly shifting life.

Elizabeth's final denouement was hardly surprising. When she began the long, final descent to death in September, Bruté tried to cheer her, "Well, they think you a little better—a hard fight—they here below praying their best to keep you with us—they above calling, I suppose, to have you happy with them." She cut through it all: "The Will—only the Will." "I hope . . . " Bruté began. And again: "Only the Will."[65]

As Mother and foundress, Elizabeth Seton was careful to hand on to her Sisters the spiritual doctrine of the Will of God in which she was now indeed an adept. "What was the first rule of our dear Savior's life?" she asked in a conference.

> You know it was to do His Father's Will. Well, then, the first end I propose in our daily work is to do the Will of God; secondly, to do it in the manner He wills it; and thirdly, to do it because it is His Will. I know what His Will is by those who direct me; whatever they bid me do, if it is ever so small in itself, is the Will of God for me. Then do it in the manner He wills it—not sewing an old thing as if it was new, or a new thing as if it was old; not fretting because the oven is too hot, or in a fuss because it is too cold. You understand—not flying and driving because you are hurried, not creeping like a snail because no one pushes you. Our dear Savior was never in extremes. The third object is to do this Will because God wills it, that is, to be ready to quit at any moment, and to do anything else we may be called to.[66]

The Church has selected this blueprint for perfection to be read in the Office of Readings on her feast. Her sister in religion, St. Catherine Labouré, echoed it in her own formula for sanctity: to do what she was given to do by her superiors, as well as she could, and for God.

Elizabeth Ann Seton held to her firm commitment to God's Will, as Protestant and Catholic, in an age that laughed at such folly and even before she was adequately instructed by orderly spiritual direction. The age was one of change and confusion, much like the present. Spawn of the Enlightenment, Voltaire's rationalism, scepticism and rejection of the supernatural and Rousseau's doctrines of the natural goodness of man and man the sole judge of his own actions held powerful sway (Elizabeth herself had been fascinated by the latter's works, especially *Emile,* which "once . . ." she confessed ruefully, "composed my *Sunday devotion*").[67] Like these two protagonists of the Enlightenment, Elizabeth's father, seemingly, and a fair number of her friends were Deists, believing vaguely in God but denying His interest in or influence over His creatures. The freedom and individuality of man were very much in the air in the wake of the American and French Revolutions. Yet, to her everlasting glory, Elizabeth refused to go with the tide, binding herself fast to the God of Revelation and His designs, tightening the bonds as she knew Him better.

Elizabeth was confident she had chosen wisely, as she assured Julia Scott: "If you knew half the real good your friend possesses, while the world thinks she is deprived of everything worth having, you would . . . allow that she has truly and really the best of it."[68] And she wrote in happy awe to Antonio Filicchi: "O Antonio, my brother dear, the ways of our God how wonderful! See my good little Sister Post and excellent Mrs. Scott *wrapped* in their blindness, and *I* in the milk and honey of Canaan already, beside the heavenly perspective."[69]

4

"PRAYER OF THE HEART"

Every saint is, indeed, must be, a man or woman of prayer. The saints' prayer is their lifeline to God, transmitting the weakness of their needs and receiving back the strength of His support, seeking light and finding enlightenment, loving and having Love Itself in return.

The exceptional prayer life of Elizabeth Seton even in childhood and adolescence has already been noted. As she settled into maturity, it became truly her way of life, and everything she did as wife and mother and society matron was impelled and guided by it. Following St. Paul with a whole-souled earnestness, whether she ate or drank or whatever else she did, she did all for the glory of God. That was not to say that her prayer was perfect; she was still largely untutored in the workings of God. However, the rightness of so much that she intuited and embraced is startling.

Elizabeth's prayer, for example, was unerringly built on the Presence of God, that practice that for centuries the Church has enjoined on eager but ignorant young novices in the religious life. "Do *I* realize it", she asked herself, "the protecting presence, the consoling grace of my Redeemer and God? He raises me from the dust to feel that I am near Him, He drives away all sorrow to fill me with His consolations. He is my *guide, my friend,* and supporter — with such a guide can I fear, with such a friend shall I not be *satisfied,* with such a supporter can I fall?"[1] It was the wide-eyed discovery of the beginner: she would not use the word *feel* to express the nearness of God in later years, nor would she then wish sorrow driven away or be filled with or even expect consolations—but it was authentic and typical of God's early tenderness toward the willing disciple.

Even more, Elizabeth's pious soul, already tried with sorrow enough, quickly suspected and responded to the starker realities beneath God's tenderness: "It is true the journey is long, the burden is heavy," she wrote in her *Spiritual Journal,* "but the Lord delivers His faithful servants from all their troubles—and sometimes, even, He allows them some hours of sweetest Peace as the earnest of eternal blessedness—Is it nothing to sleep serene under His guardian wing, to awake [to] the brightness of the glorious sun with renewed strength and renewed blessings?" She was beginning to feel the sting anew; it had not gone away, and she was counting her blessings almost defensively, but in the next breath there is a burst of insight that pierces to the heart of prayer and the spiritual life: "To be blessed with the power of instant communion with the Father of our spirits, the sense of His presence—the influences of His love". How much that one word *instant* reveals of her progress! How close already her communion with her only Beloved! How wholly her life is already influenced, molded and guided by His love is in the understanding and acceptance of what follows: "To be assured of that love is enough to tie us faithfully to Him, and while we have fidelity to Him all the surrounding cares and contradictions of this life are but cords of mercy to bind us faster to Him who will hereafter make even their remembrance to vanish in the reality of our eternal felicity."[2] Her perception of the purpose and effectiveness of trials and tribulations would not be more unerring on her deathbed.

Elizabeth wrote these words on the Eve of the Ascension, and her entry for the feast itself has the impulsiveness of love and the humility of patience: "Oh, that my soul could go up with my blessed Lord—that it might be *where He is also*—Thy Will be done—my time is in Thy hands. . . . Raise us up by a life of faith with Thee."[3]

Elizabeth's "instant communication with the Father" so early in her life is probably the greatest of all her blessings, for in divine union everything is contained. Although far from as common among creatures as it should be, the mystery of divine union is simple and uncomplicated, even easy. The problem is the complexity of fallen human nature, which sees difficulties everywhere and insists upon doing things its own way, thus posing the greatest difficulty of all. "How pitiful is it", Elizabeth lamented to her religious daughters, "to put our devotion in a multitude of prayers too often repeated, without attention to what we say, and scarcely thinking to whom we are speaking . . . without listening to God, who would receive so much more glory from even the shortest adorations proceeding from the heart. The least sentence — 'I adore you, my God; I love you, my God; I submit wholly to Your adorable Will' — would be so much more agreeable to Him."[4]

Elizabeth's own uncomplicated docility sees this wondrous mystery of divine union as simply "instant communication" in her youth, and as "the simple look of the heart to God" in her older years of spiritual wisdom. Little has changed. Even her urging it upon her Sisters is gentle: This "simple look of the heart to God", she assures them, "draws and unites it to Him in a sentiment of peace and confidence, the fruit of His goodness to those who love Him".[5] It is common practice, one with which they are familiar in varying degrees, she insinuates encouragingly, "Those less practiced in this heavenly exercise must humbly beg Him to advance them in it, that *the look of their soul* may be continually towards Him, and when they find it has been sometime diverted from this adorable object, it must say to itself, 'What have we been doing, where were we so long without thinking of our God?' "[6]

Elizabeth herself was truly an adept by now, as she once artlessly revealed to her director: "I have not done as much community work of hearing, seeing and speaking in the last 6 months as this day, with a heart as 'still as a calm at sea'. . . . Now *sleep* with *Him* from whom I think I have not parted a minute since I saw you."[7] Easy as this unbroken union seemed, she knew it was not and admitted in an instruction "that God does not grant to all the facility of thinking of Him continually though all can *frequently* do it if they will".[8]

As always, Elizabeth did not demand of her Sisters "six impossible things before breakfast", but patiently showed them how to master what may have seemed impossible to them at first. "A simple remembrance of the presence of God *in us*" was a starting point. It was "particularly recommended, by many saints," she said, "not to exclude the view of His presence everywhere, but to call our attention to our own interior, and help us the more easily to be recollected". The "trial . . . of much exterior occupation" could be an obstacle, she conceded, but such occupation did not include the work they had come to religious life to do: "It must be repeated there is no greater error", she insisted, "than to imagine that the very employments which God Himself gives us shall force us to forget Him while we are engaged in them"; to forestall objection she resorted to practical experience: "In the most hurried time, we speak to those who are round us, talk of the work we are doing, and yet cannot remember *Him* who is so powerful and ready to help us through it."⁹

"The love of talk", Elizabeth reminded as well, "distracts all the powers of our soul from God, and fills them with earthly objects and impressions, like a vessel of water which cannot be clear and settled while you are continually stirring the earthy particles from the bottom." And, "*self-love* is directly opposed to charity and an insuperable obstacle to our union with God". Above all, she implored, "be not like those who are before Him like a slave, and wait the end of their duty of obligation to find their liberty and pleasure in leaving Him".

Nonetheless, they were to be proud of their calling to the active apostolate: "If the contemplative Magdalenes enjoy more sweetness, they don't possess more merit", Elizabeth stated bluntly. "One who runs over a whole city carrying God in his thoughts, is much more pleasing in His sight, than another who lets his thoughts run about while they are kneeling in an oratory."¹⁰

After all explanation and warning, however, Elizabeth returned to what she had learned as a young Protestant matron: "The best means to increase the *love* of God in our heart which would make the practice of the presence of God so easy to us, is to consider

Him as our *Tender Father.*" Everything, then, will fall in place, "*Our look of love at Him draws back a look of love on us,* and His divine look enkindles that fire of love in us which makes us remember Him continually."[11]

"Fire of love" is an expression used routinely but seldom experienced. Elizabeth Seton knew what it meant when she used it. "Nothing in our state of clouds and veils I can see so plainly, as how the saints died of love and joy," she once exclaimed to Bruté, "since I, so wretched and truly miserable, can only read word after word of the blessed 83rd and 41st Psalms in unutterable feelings ever to our God through the thousand pressings and overflowings—God—God—God, that the supreme delight, that He is God, and to open the mouth and heart wide that He may fill it."[12] She understood the necessity of letting go of oneself, of giving way completely to God, of immersing oneself in Him—"He is more within us than we are ourselves",[13] was the way she expressed it—and the blessed reward of His love and peace flooding every recess of her soul.

Elizabeth expressed it even more fully in a supreme definition of the Presence of God that is also as supreme a definition of prayer: "A respectful *Silence* before the divine majesty, a silence which the great St. Denis calls the HIGHEST PRAISE."[14] (More recently, Pope John Paul II has called this silence "the greatest prayer".) "This tumultuous Silence," St. Elizabeth Ann continues, "when proceeding from our impressions of His perfections and greatness, is the most suitable homage we can offer Him, losing ourselves in His divine presence, in our deep abasement having no desire or wish but to be conformed to His Will and wholly sacrificed to Him."[15]

It is not surprising that she who was the most devoted of mothers, wives, relatives and friends should especially descry the ones she loved in God and share the discovery, so comforting to weak humanity, with others. "The accidents of life separate us from our dearest friends, but let us not despair", Elizabeth cautioned her Sisters. "God is like a looking glass in which souls see each other." It was a bold but penetrating grasp of God's simplicity and

omniscience thus to see in them the communion of saints, for it is
evident that it was friends of God she meant. "The more we are
united to Him by love, the nearer we are to those who belong to
Him", she continued. "Jesus Christ encompasses all places, and all
His members center in Him; we need but prostrate at His feet to
find them. They may be hidden from the eyes of our body, but
not from the eyes of our soul of Faith."[16]

Elizabeth's prayer, quite naturally, grew, intertwining itself with
her daily life and its every action and event. It would be a dunning
of the obvious to search out every thread, but it can be rewarding
to trace the pattern of prayer in major crises of her life in all its
effulgent power.

Throughout the terrifying ordeal of her husband's last illness in
the *lazaretto,* prayer was Elizabeth's only resource. From the very
first day it was her "trust in God . . . that will carry us on. *He* is
our all indeed. My eyes smart so much with crying, wind and
fatigue, that I must close them and lift up my heart."[17] When, on
the second day, "the matin bells awakened my soul to its most
painful regrets", she despaired that her "agony of sorrow . . .
would not find relief even in prayer"; but "I . . . came to my senses
and reflected that I was offending my only Friend and Resource in
my misery, and voluntarily shutting out from my soul the only
consolation it could receive. Pleading for mercy and strength
brought peace."[18] This first taste of peace in a forlorn situation
quickly communicated itself to Elizabeth's frightened little daughter Anna Maria: "Ann with a flood of tears said her prayers and
soon forgot her sorrows; and it seemed", the mother recognized
anew, "as if opening my prayer-book and bending my knees was
the signal for my soul to find rest".[19] This blessed tranquility
reached almost an ecstasy of divine union as the horrible hours
and days dragged on and on. Asked whether she would not want
some older person with her during the ordeal—"Oh, no! What
had I to fear? And what *had* I to fear? I laid down as if to rest, that
he [William] might not be uneasy. Listened all night: sometimes
by the fire, sometimes lying down, sometimes thought the breathing
stopped, and sometimes alarmed by its heaviness, and I kissed his

poor face to feel if it was cold. Well, was I alone? Dear, indulgent *Father!* Could I be alone while clinging fast to Thee in continual prayer of thanksgiving . . . ?"[20]

Prayer, her own and her friends', effected Elizabeth's conversion, brought her, she acknowledged, "to the light of Thy truth, notwithstanding every affection of my heart and power of my will was opposed to it".[21]

Prayer established Elizabeth's religious community and her school. "[Father Babade] applies to me the Psalm in our Vespers: *The barren woman shall be the joyful mother of children,* and tells me to repeat it continually," she wrote Cecilia Seton, "which you must do with me, my darling."[22] And she informed Antonio Filicchi: "Every morning at the Divine Sacrifice, I offer (as I know they [the Sulpician Fathers] do also) the whole success to Him whose blessed Will alone can sanctify and make it fruitful."[23] But the most startling manifestation of the power of prayer at work was attested to by Father William Dubourg:

> An insurmountable obstacle stood in the way of this project; this was the absolute want of pecuniary resources to lay the foundation of this new Society. They [himself and Mrs. Seton] resolved to pray jointly to God to remove this obstacle. One morning, in the year 1808, Mrs. Seton called upon her director [himself] and told him, at the risk of being considered a visionary, she felt obliged to disclose to him *what Our Lord, in a clear and intelligible voice, said to her after Communion:* "Go," said He to her, "address yourself to Mr. Cooper; he will give you what is necessary to commence the establishment."[24]

That evening Samuel Cooper, independently and knowing nothing of the project, asked Dubourg why nothing was done for the education of women. Apprised of Mrs. Seton's intentions and the obstacle in their way, he replied, "I have ten thousand dollars which I can give you for this purpose."[25]

Once Elizabeth Seton and her first little band of Sisters began the religious life, they did so in the spirit of profound prayer. The very first day they sealed their consecration at early Mass at

St. Joseph's Church in the village of Emmitsburg, all going to confession and receiving their Lord. The next day they began that "order of regularity" that Mother Seton insisted from the first "cannot be skipped over here":[26] rising at five o'clock, morning prayers and meditation before—in the earliest months—walking to Mass at St. Joseph's or St. Mary's on the mountain, reciting the Joyful Mysteries of the Rosary on the way and the Sorrowful Mysteries coming back; the day went on with Scripture and *The Spiritual Combat* read at meals, examens of conscience, visits to the Blessed Sacrament, spiritual reading, the final Mysteries of the Rosary, work and recreation—all in common with one heart and one soul lifted up to God.[27]

St. Elizabeth Ann's personal approach to prayer was, as one would expect, in complete agreement with the masters of theology and the spiritual life. She believed, first of all, in God's providence and solicitude for the creatures of His love. "God is with us", she wrote staunchly amid the sufferings of the *lazaretto.* "If the wind . . . that now almost puts out my light and blows on my William through every crevice, and over our chimney like loud thunder, could come from any but His command; or if the circumstances which placed us in so forlorn a situation were not guided by His hand—miserable indeed would be our case."[28] And again, "If I could forget my God one moment at these times, I should go mad."[29]

The next step, to God's power and willingness to intervene in human concerns, was easy, and Elizabeth's belief as firm. "God will not forsake me, Antonio", she assured her "dear Filicchi" in the agony of her conversion to the Catholic Faith. "I know that He will unite me to His flock; and, although my Faith is unsettled, I am assured that He will not disappoint my hope which is fixed on His own word, that He will not despise the humble, contrite heart."[30]

This same confidence was still fresh and firm a dozen years later in a letter of promise to Bruté, who had just been named President of St. Mary's in Baltimore: "Yes, our dear President, you will, you shall have prayers plenty of these most innocent hearts [her daughters and the Sisters], and I say so often *I have a Jesus to offer* —and look up *confidently*—He will not leave you who have left all for Him, nor leave you in weakness while loading yourself for His sake. No, no, no, G—*He will not.* So we press the crucifix closer on the heart, and trust *all.* "[31] What a bold assertion: *"I have a Jesus to offer"!* Yet, she was quite right. Jesus has given Himself to those He redeemed that they might offer Him continuously to the Father. It takes a saint, an intimate, to say it so bluntly. In speaking to Antonio of "unsettled faith" and "the humble, contrite heart", Elizabeth put her finger on what can weaken or even obstruct the efficacy of prayer: the dispositions of the one who prays. Her own dispositions, at the time, may indeed have been imperfect, for Bishop Carroll worried whether "the tears she sheds and the prayers she offers to heaven are purely for God's sake and arise solely from compunction for sin, and are unmixed with any alloy of worldly respects or inordinate solicitude for the attainment of some worldly purpose."[32] In later years the saint herself added to the list of bad dispositions "useless thoughts, inconsiderate words, expressions of natural feelings and changes of temper", which she saw as stopping "the operation of divine grace, too often indeed even to grieving the divine Spirit and sending Him away".[33]

Elizabeth insisted upon purity of intention and relied upon it to cleanse and clothe those daily actions that were themselves prayers, "going as you know to meet everybody in the grace of the moment, which we can never know till we find the humor and temper of the one we are to meet with—the many mistakes all swallowed and comforted by *intention,* intention, intention, our true peace and security with our Beloved".[34]

Another delightful quality of prayer and good living Elizabeth urged was *cheerfulness.* A surprising quality at first glance, but not in one of her happy enthusiasm. "Cheerfulness", she is not afraid to say, "prepares a glorious mind for all the noblest acts of religion—love, adoration, praise and every union with Our God, as also for duties, charity, happy zeal, useful concern for our neighbor, and all those acts of PIETY which should improve cheerfulness, and dispose the poor soul to joyful serenity—resting all upon infinite goodness!

Thrice infinite goodness of our Adored and Beloved."[35] Would that all who love God reflected His holy good humor as well! The *duties,* as Elizabeth Seton insisted, along with the satisfying consolations. How much less holding back there would be in the frightened and doubtful.

Elizabeth herself was the apostle of cheerfulness, as in this note to her friend George Weis concerning the use of holy water, which she used "every day and night . . . in the morning to defend from danger—at night to efface the errors of the day. You must allow that enthusiasts have a region of happiness where the wise ones do not enter; or if they did, they would find a sort of Greek they would not understand."[36] To poke fun, thus, at the pompous is the best way to deflate them, like the ludicrous plight of the liberated young student of the Sorbonne who discovered that the old man he was baiting for saying the Rosary was Louis Pasteur. The world needs the spirit of fun of an Elizabeth Seton to rout the sober "intellectuals" who find sacramentals highly suspect and seem to have banished the Miraculous Medal and the Christian mothers who guarded their households from the threat of lightning with a blessed candle and Elizabeth's holy water or soothed the bumps and cuts of childhood with the sign of the Cross on the wounds with their wedding rings.

God's interests always had priority in Elizabeth's prayers. When her son William and friend Bruté were on the high seas in constant danger from storms, pirates and ships of warring nations, she asked, "What is the worst and the worst that can happen to the *dearest,* Death? And what of that? But the poor 'pupil' who may make shipwreck of his dear eternal interest, or the one hand less to hold the chalice—*there the point,* and the *immense interests.*"[37] This zeal for the Kingdom embraced the whole world, as she confided to her older son on the cessation of hostilities with Britain in 1815: "Your poor mother looks only at souls. I see neither American or English, but souls redeemed and lost."[38]

The final dogged quality of Mother Seton's prayer was perseverance. She had learned it from Filippo Filicchi during the frustrations of her struggle to believe. " 'What must I do, my dear Filicchi?' I hear you say"—so he had written—"Pray, pray incessantly, pray with fervor and confidence. . . . You cannot ask without something being given you; you cannot knock and find the door always shut; you cannot seek never to find. Sincerity, confidence and perseverance in prayer; calmness and tranquility of mind; courage and resolution in heart; a perfect resignation to Providence—you cannot fail to succeed."[39] Elizabeth applied the lesson unflaggingly until she had reached the haven of sure faith and continued to apply it afterward under the abuse of false-hearted family and friends, by prayer and action buoyed up by Antonio Filicchi—"Courage and perseverance!"[40]—by Bishop Carroll urging the same, by Father Francis Matignon, who promised that "your perseverance and the help of grace will finish in you the work which God has commenced".[41] And Bishop John Cheverus, in the travail of establishing the community, expressed the same serene confidence in the outcome of her persevering will.

It is obvious from these and other examples of St. Elizabeth Seton's combined prayer and holy action that she was certainly not so naïve as to expect prayer to effect everything or anything without human effort. She once reported to Bruté:

Gave our Reverend J. Hickey a scolding he will remember. The congregation so crowded yesterday, and so many strangers—to whom he gave a sermon so evidently lazy; and answered this morning:

"I did not trouble myself about it, Ma'am."

"Oh, sir, that awakens my anger. Do you remember a priest holds the honor of God on his lips. Do you not trouble to spread His fire He wishes so much enkindled? If you will not study and prepare while young, what when you are old? There is a mother's lesson."

"But, prayer . . . "

"Yes, prayer—and *preparation,* too."[42]

This indefatigable Mother once jotted down for her Sisters what really amounts to a guarantee of prayer's efficacy; there is nothing magical about the formula, but, if followed faithfully and lovingly, it cannot fail with God. "There *are three* particular points on which God will always listen to us with the most pleasure", the saint wrote with calm certainty, "the declarations of our *sorrow for sin, our faith, love and hope* on the mysteries of Redemption, *our gratitude* for His deliverance from the many dangers of our *past* life, and present desires of better service and fidelity."[43] Here, indeed, is the way, the path of a soul who truly loves God and to whom God listens.

Elizabeth's overall grasp of the nature of prayer and its function as a never-failing lifeline between God and the soul is beautifully expressed in an instruction written for fifteen-year-old Cecilia Seton, drawn by Elizabeth's example to the Catholic Church when Elizabeth was but a few months in that Faith. "We must pray literally without ceasing—without ceasing; in every occurrence and employment of our lives", she exhorted the child.

You know I mean that prayer of the heart which is independent of place or situation, or which is, rather, a habit of lifting up the heart to God, as in a constant communication with Him.

As, for instance, when you go to your studies, you look up to Him with sweet complacency, and think: O Lord how worthless is this knowledge, if it were not for the enlightening my mind and improving it to Thy service; or for being more useful to my fellow-creatures, and enabled to fill the part Thy Providence may appoint me.

When going into society or mixing with company, appeal to Him who sees your heart, and knows how much rather you would devote every hour to Him; but say: "Dear Lord! You have placed me here, and I must yield to them whom You have placed me in subjection to—O keep my heart from all that would separate me from Thee."

When you are excited to impatience, think for a moment how much more reason God has to be angry with you, than you can have for anger against any human being; and yet how constant is His patience and forbearance.

And in every disappointment, great or small, let your dear heart fly direct to Him, your dear Savior, throwing yourself in His arms for refuge against every pain and sorrow. He never will leave you or forsake you."[44]

5

"OUR LORD AND OUR LADY"

Two devotions especially captured Elizabeth Seton's soul. The first was devotion to the Mass and Holy Eucharist; the second, devotion to the Mother of God. Her predilection for both is hardly extraordinary, since both have a preeminence in the Catholic Church, the first being, of course, the very heart of its faith and mission, and the second a logical recognition of the essential role Mary plays in that faith and mission. What is arresting is that Elizabeth had an unusual devotion to "the sacrament" when she was a Protestant (she could not be expected to have devotion to Mary when her Episcopal Communion did not); and that she who was truly the Mother of the Catholic Church in the United States had deep love for the two devotions that have ever been dear to American Catholics.

Elizabeth seems to have had a belief of some kind in a Real Presence of Christ in the Protestant Episcopal Sacrament. On a terrible Sunday of trial that broke the dam of her doubts and swept her into the true Faith, she described for Amabilia Filicchi how she went "trembling to communion, half-dead with the inward struggle when they said the BODY AND BLOOD OF CHRIST. . . . I remember in my old prayer-book of former edition, when I was a child, it was not as now; said to be *spiritually* taken and received."[1] She was quite right. When the newly formed Protestant Episcopal Church in America held its first General Convention in Philadelphia in 1789, it revised the sentence in the

Anglican Book of Common Prayer "the Body and Blood of Christ . . . are verily and indeed taken and received by the faithful in the Lord's Supper", to read "spiritually taken and received".[2] Certainly, then, the Anglican sacrament was not for Elizabeth merely a symbolic memorial. That it was not as well the wholly objective Presence of Catholic belief is suggested by the sense of new revelation in what she was to learn in Italy.

Elizabeth's Protestant devotion to the Sacrament was, nevertheless, deep and abiding. It has been noted that she seized upon it as "the seal of that Covenant which I trust will not be broken in life nor in death, in time nor in eternity".[3] When she received Communion, "her teeth chattered against the cup of wine in an ecstasy of trembling awe", and her sister-in-law Rebecca Seton and friend Catherine Dupleix used to join her in asking the sexton for the remnants of the sacramental wine that they might receive again.[4] Elizabeth reminded Rebecca Seton of their rather extravagant devotion in retailing Catholic practice in Livorno, which evidently delighted her:

> How often you and I used to give the sigh, and you would press your arm in mine of a Sunday evening and say, *"No more until next Sunday"*, as we turned from the Church door which closed on us (unless a prayer day was given out in the week). Well, here they go to church at four every morning, if they please. And you know we were laughed at for running from one church to the other, *Sacrament Sundays*, that we might receive as often as we could. Well, here people that love God and live a good, regular life, can go (though many do not [do] it), yet they can go every day.[5]

The doling out of the Sacrament was a real deprivation, and Elizabeth was forced to devotional extravagance to compensate for it. "Poor fool, no Sacrament Sunday," she noted in her *Dear Remembrances*, "most reverently drank on my knees behind the library door the little cup of wine and tears to represent what I so much desired".[6] God surely did not laugh at the symbolic remembrance lashed with the tears of yearning love. There was another attempt to conjure up the Sacrament, in a time of dire need.

There can be no doubt that Elizabeth's constant yearning for sacramental union with Jesus as an Episcopalian prepared the way for the eagerness, despite a tentative, natural holding back, with which she reached out to the Catholic doctrine of the Eucharist. With her first known entrance into a Catholic church—*La Santissima Annunziata* in Florence—there is a sense of homecoming: "Forgetting Mrs. F[ilicchi], companions, and all the surrounding scene," she told Rebecca, "I sank on my knees in the first place I found vacant, and shed a torrent of tears at the recollection of how long I had been a stranger in the house of my God, and the accumulated sorrow that had separated me from it. I need not tell you that I said our dear service with my whole soul, as far as in its agitation I could recollect."[7] However unconsciously, a sense of a Presence was stealing into her soul, for she felt "delight in seeing old men and women, young women and all sorts of people kneeling promiscuously about the altar, as inattentive to us and other passengers as if we were not there . . . everyone is so intent on their prayers and Rosary that it is very immaterial what a stranger does."[8] The "stranger" she then was turned wistful in the church of San Firenze as she "saw a young priest unlock his little chapel, with that composed and equal eye as if his soul had entered before him. My heart would willingly have followed after."[9] That heart was itself unlocked by the exuberance of *San Lorenzo,* unlike anything she had known in the plain places of worship at home. The natural exuberance of her soul—the "wildness", as she called it—so long suppressed by accustomed forms of staid worship, responded: "A sensation of delight struck me so forcibly that as I approached the great altar, formed all of the most precious stones and marbles that could be produced, 'My soul doth magnify the Lord, my spirit rejoices in God my Savior', came in my mind with a fervor which absorbed every other feeling."[10]

The real moment of truth came in the Shrine of Montenero, high above Livorno overlooking the harbor and the open sea. At the very moment of the elevation of the Host, a young English tourist leaned towards Elizabeth and explained in a loud, rude whisper, "This is what they call their *Real Presence.*" The words were a shock of grace: "My very heart trembled with shame and sorrow for his unfeeling interruption of their sacred adoration", was her first, well-bred and at the same time sense-of-religious-outrage reaction. But then: "Involuntarily I bent from him to the pavement, and thought secretly on the words of St. Paul, with starting tears, 'They discern not the Lord's Body.'" It was an instinctive, unwitting gesture of adoration. The moment passed, but it triggered a spate of confused questions: "The next thought was, how should they eat and drink their very damnation for not *discerning* it, if indeed it was not *there?* Yet how should it be *there?* And how did *He* breathe my soul in me? And how, and how a hundred other things I know nothing about? I am a *mother,* so the mother's thought came also. How was my God a little babe in the first stage of His mortal existence *in Mary?* But I lost these thoughts in my babes at home, which I daily long for more and more."[*][11]

No matter, the iron had struck deep into Elizabeth's soul. Weeks later she was writing her "soul's sister", Rebecca:

> How happy would we be, if we believed what these dear souls believe: that they *possess God* in the Sacrament, and that He remains in their churches and is carried to them when they are sick! Oh, my! When they carry the Blessed Sacrament under my window, while I feel the full loneliness and sadness of my case, I cannot stop the tears at the thought. My God, how happy would I be, even so far away from all so dear, if I could find You in the church as they do (for there is a chapel in the very house of Mrs. F[ilicchi]) how many things I would say to You in the sorrows of my heart and the sins of my life!

[*] Elizabeth gives another account of this important incident in her *Dear Remembrances:* "My first entrance in the Church of B.V.M. of Montenero at Leghorn. At the elevation, a young Englishman near me, forgetting decency, whispered 'This is their real presence.' The shame I felt at his whisper, and the quick thought, *If Our Lord is not there, why did the Apostle threaten? — How can he blame for not discerning the Lord's Body, if it is not there? — How should they for whom He has died eat and drink their damnation (as says the Protestant text), if the Blessed Sacrament is but a piece of bread?"*

The sacramental Lord she had always loved was drawing her to His fullness, and finally: "The other day, in a moment of excessive distress, I fell on my knees without thinking when the Blessed Sacrament passed by, and cried in an agony to God *to bless me,* if He was *there* — that my whole soul desired only Him."[12]

The ache is even more poignant in Elizabeth's *Dear Remembrances:* "The anguish of heart when the Blessed Sacrament would be passing the street, at the thought, *Was I the only one He did not bless?*"[13] It must have been anguish indeed for one so committed to Jesus, to wonder whether she was outcast, ignored by Him. The pain was nearly unbearable "the day He passed my window when, prostrate on the floor, I looked up to the Blessed Virgin, appealing to her that, as the Mother of God, she *must* pity me". She desperately wanted more than pity. She had come to the point where her prayer to Mary was "to obtain from Him that blessed Faith of these happy souls around me — rising after many sighs and tears — the little prayer book Mrs. Amabilia had given Annina was under my eye, which fell on St. Bernard's prayer to the Blessed Virgin — How earnestly I said it, how many thoughts of the happiness of those who possessed this blessed Faith of Jesus still on earth with them." *That* is what drew her, what fascinated her: the thought of having this Lord she loved so dearly actually *with* her at all times — if she could only believe *that!* She had already worked out what it would mean to her: "How I should enjoy to encounter every misery of life with the heavenly consolation of speaking heart to heart with Him in His Tabernacles, and the security of finding Him in His churches." It was why she had special "reverence and love to Mrs. Amabilia Filicchi when she came home from communion".[14]

These Filicchis, every one of them, were her God-appointed saviors. A double family wedding celebrated by Amabilia's brother Nicóla Baragazzi brought "impressions of awful reverence . . . and full continuance of it when he visited our chamber [Anna sick] in his robe of ceremony after the marriage of his brother and sister".[15] Like the splendor of the churches, the very vestments of the liturgy were doing their work of teaching, of drawing the eye of the beholder to the Creator of all.

Later yet, on the eve of Elizabeth's departure for home, her mind had settled and her soul lay open awaiting the gift of faith with a poignant hunger for eucharistic union. "Oh, my soul, how solemn was that offering!" she wrote of her last Mass in Livorno. "For a blessing on our voyage, for my dear ones, my sisters and all so dear to me—and, more than all, for the souls of my dear husband and father"—all one in the communion of saints—"earnestly our desires ascended with the blessed sacrifice, that they might find acceptance through Him who gave Himself for us"—how well she understood the divine ladder of sacrificial praise and grace ascending and descending—"Earnestly we desired to be united with Him, and would gladly encounter all the sorrows before us, to be partakers of that blessed Body and Blood. Oh, my God, spare and pity me."[16] The hunger was stark in a last line scribbled to Rebecca Seton: "My Savior! My God! Antonio and his wife—their separation in God and Communion! Poor I, *not.* But did I not beg Him to give me their Faith, and promise him *all* in return for such a gift? Little Ann and I had only strange tears of joy and grief."[17]

Back in New York, Elizabeth's quest for the ultimate gift became a real struggle to the death, unnerved and unraveled as she now became with the polemic treatises forced on her by well-meaning friends on both sides; however, the cry of her heart still rang clear. When Bishop Carroll wrote to sustain her, she assured Antonio Filicchi: "*The Bishop's letter* has been held to my heart on my knees, beseeching God to enlighten me to see the truth unmixed with doubts and hesitations. I read the promises given to St. Peter and the Sixth Chapter John"—the explicit promise of the Eucharist—"every day, and then ask God, can I offend Him by believing those express words?"[18] And she told his wife, Amabilia, that she had gone to her old trysting place St. Paul's for reasons of "peace, and persuasion about proprieties, etc. . . . Yet, I got in a side pew which turned my face toward the Catholic Church in the next street, and found myself twenty times speaking to the Blessed Sacrament *there,* instead of looking at the naked altar where I was, or minding the routine of prayers."[19] She lingered outside Catholic St. Peter's, longing "every day to visit my Savior there and pour out my soul before Him".[20]

How happy the Ash Wednesday of 1805, when at last Elizabeth could write exultantly to Mrs. Filicchi:

> A day of days for me, Amabilia. I have been where?—to the Church of St. Peter with the cross on top instead of a weathercock! That is mischievous—but I mean I have been to what is called here among so many churches *the Catholic Church*. When I turned the corner of the street it is in—"Here, my God, I go," I said, *"heart all to You"*. Entering it, how the heart died away as it were in silence before the little tabernacle and the great Crucifixion over it. "Ah, my God, here let me rest", said I—and down the head on the bosom and the knees on the bench.[21]

If there were any doubt that Elizabeth Seton's instinctive turning to the Sacrament of the Eucharist from her earliest Protestant days, her grasp of it even then as the heart of the Church, her eager opening to the full-blown eucharistic doctrine of the Catholic Church, had exerted the strongest pull of all to that true Faith, the ecstasy of her first Communion dispels it in an instant. "ANNUNCIATION DAY", she informed Amabilia. "I shall be made one with Him who said, 'Unless you eat My Flesh and drink My Blood you can have no part with Me.'" She had accepted "Sixth Chapter John" with simple, grateful belief. "I count the days and hours. Yet a few more of hope and expectation, and then— How bright the sun, these morning walks of preparation. Deep snow or smooth ice, all to me the same. I see nothing but the little bright cross on St. Peter's steeple."[22] And finally, the long, long awaited day:

> 25th MARCH. At last Amabilia, at last GOD IS MINE AND I AM HIS! Now, let all go its round—*I have received Him.* The awful impressions of the evening before, fears of not having done all to prepare, and yet, even the transports of confidence and hope in His Goodness. MY GOD! To the last breath of life will I not remember this night of watching for morning dawn; the fearful, beating heart so pressing to be gone; the long walk to town; but

every step counted, nearer that street, then nearer that tabernacle, then nearer the moment He would enter the poor, poor little dwelling so all His own—and when He did, the first thought I remember was: "Let God arise, let His enemies be scattered!"— for it seemed to me my King had come to take His throne, and instead of the humble, tender welcome I had expected to give Him, it was but a triumph of joy and gladness that the deliverer was come and my defense and shield and strength and salvation made mine for this world and the next.[23]

Another contradiction, but a glorious one: not what she had carefully and prayerfully planned, but what He wished. He knew well, after all she had been through, what favor to bestow. It had the victory and exaltation of Easter in it, not only for the spent, humble soul of His beloved and elected one but also for His people whom she would inflame with His love.

And, tuned now as Elizabeth was to *her* Beloved, she knew how to respond: "Now, then, all the excesses of my heart found their play and danced with more fervor—no, must not say that— but perhaps, almost with as much as the royal prophet's before his ark. For I was far richer than he, and more honored than he could ever be. Now, the point is for the fruits." She was not so lost in heavenly enjoyment that she could not discern its purpose. Nor did she fail to perceive that this first eucharistic encounter had worked an irreversible change in her soul that was both the promise and the wellspring of constant future spiritual growth: "So far, truly I feel all the powers of my soul held fast by Him who came with so much majesty to take possession of His little poor kingdom."[24] And she began to prepare for "an Easter Communion . . . in my green pastures, amidst the refreshing fountains for which I thirsted truly"[25]—chief of which was "the Divine Sacrifice, so commanding and yet already so familiar for all my wants and necessities. That speaks for itself, and I am all at home in it."[26]

Years later, the exquisite wonder of Elizabeth's "first communion in the Church of God" was still a fresh delight in her soul as she jotted down her *Dear Remembrances* because "it would be such

INGRATITUDE to die without noting them". "Hours counted, the watch of the heart, panting for the supreme happiness it had so long desired—the Secret"—there was, then, as might be expected between two such ardent lovers, a communication no one will ever know, nor should—"The mystery of Benediction—heavenly delight, bliss—inconceivable to angels, no word for that—Faith burning." The words themselves seem to gasp and pant in an effort to express the inexpressible. "The lively hope that since He had done so much He would at last admit so poor a creature to Himself *forever*"—she had not forgotten what she had learned with the self-abandonment of the covenant in 1802, that this true Eucharist now fully attained was the pledge of everlasting life—"The two miles walk back with the treasure of my soul—first kiss and blessing on my 5 Darlings, bringing *such a Master* to our little dwelling." As she knew enough instinctively to venerate the person of Amabilia Filicchi when she returned home after Communion, Elizabeth, now the bearer, rejoiced in sharing her blessed burden with her children and, through the attentive practice of charity, with the neighbor: "Now the quiet, satisfied heart in the thousand encounters of the cross embraced so cordially, but so watchfully, to preserve peace with *all*."[27]

Once safe in God's green pastures, Elizabeth's impish nature reasserted itself with the freedom of the children of God, even in something so awesomely sacred. " 'Faith for all defects supplies, and sense is lost in mystery'—'Here the faithful rest secure, while God can vouch, and Faith insure.'[28] But you would sometimes enjoy, through mischief," she wrote gaily to Amabilia, "if you could just know the foolish things that pass my brain after so much wonderful knowledge as I have been taking in it, about idol worshipping, etc., etc.,—even in the sacred moments of the Elevation, my heart will say, half-serious, 'Dare I worship You, Adored Savior?' But He has proved to me well enough *there* what He is, and I can say with even more transports than St. Thomas, 'My Lord and my God!' " Then the impatience of the convert, forgetting for the moment what she had had to suffer to believe, burst forth:

Truly, it is a greater mystery how souls for whom He has done such *incomprehensible things* should shut themselves out by incredulity from His best of all gifts, this Divine Sacrifice and Holy Eucharist—refusing to believe in spiritual and heavenly order of things *that Word* which spoke and created the whole natural order, recreating through succession of ages for the body, and yet He cannot be believed to recreate for the soul. I see more mystery in this blindness of redeemed souls than in any of the mysteries proposed in His Church. With what grateful and unspeakable joy and reverence I adore the daily renewed virtue of that Word by which we possess Him in our blessed Mass and Communion![29]

That He was Elizabeth's possession, indeed, her bulwark, in His glorious Sacrament was evident in her gentle turning aside of Antonio's insistence on her settling with her family in Italy for the peace of their religion: "Since I hope always to find the morning *Mass in America,* it matters little what can happen through the few successive days I may have to live."[30] She was already leaning wholly on this sacramental strength. "From circumstances of particular impressions on my mind," she told Antonio, "I have been obliged to watch it so carefully and keep so near the Fountain Head, that I have been three times to Communion since you left me, not to influence my faith, but to keep peace in my soul, which without this heavenly resource would be agitated and discomposed by the frequent assaults which, in my immediate situation, are naturally made on my feelings."[31]

Elizabeth knew interior assaults as well, and the remedy: "The heart down—discouraged at the constant failure in good resolution; so soon disturbed by trifles; so little interior recollection and forgetfulness of His constant presence. The reproaches of disobedience to the little ones much more applicable to myself. So many Communions and confessions with so little fruit often suggest the idea of lessening them—to fly from the fountain while in danger of dying from thirst! But, in a moment, He lifts up the soul from the dust."[32] It was the constant struggle for perfection with its relapses and gains.

Elizabeth's comparison of her "disobedience" to that of the children was not a passing thought. She combined the intuitions of mother and saint to plan her way to holiness. "Beloved Kate, I will take you, then, for my pattern", she confided to her *Spiritual Journal,*

> and try to please Him as you to please me. To grieve with a like tenderness when I displease *Him,* to obey and mind His voice as you do mine. To do my work as neatly and exactly as you do yours, grieve to lose sight of Him for a moment, fly with joy to meet Him, fear He should go and leave me even when I sleep—this is the lesson of love you set me. And when I have seemed to be angry, without petulance or obstinacy you silently and steadily try to accomplish my wish, I will say: "Dearest Lord, give me grace to copy well this lovely image of my duty to Thee."[33]

Through her children, too, she deepened her understanding of and participation in the communion of saints: "Received the longing Desire of my soul", she recorded, "and my dearest Anna, too. The bonds of nature and grace all twined together. The parent offers the child, the child the parent, and both are united in the source of their being, and rest together on redeeming love."[34] This unseen but constant communion of souls in the Sacrament was, again, her rebuttal of the fear "to go among strangers" as she entered on her holy exile in Baltimore—"One sweet Sacrifice will reunite my soul with all who offer it."[35] It indeed reunited her with the very roots of her faith! "Imagine", she conjured up for Cecilia Seton, "twenty priests all with the devotion of saints, clothed in white, accompanied by the whole troop of young seminarians in surplices also, all in order surrounding the Blessed Sacrament exposed, singing the hymn of the Resurrection. When they come to the words, 'Peace be to all here', it seems as if Our Lord is again acting over the scene that passed with the assembled disciples."[36]

As might be expected, Elizabeth's intense love for the Holy Eucharist, so carefully nurtured and joyously indulged, could only deepen with the years. Father Bruté wrote with a kind of sacred envy after her death: "May my heart, my soul, know the grace and prove the grace of the Holy Sacrament of my Jesus as Mother did."[37] As might be expected, too, her love generated extraordinary insights reserved for the divine intimate. Thus, she communicated to Bruté a new understanding of the Beatitude "Blessed are the poor in spirit" and God's predilection for the lowly: "A most precious Communion, preceded by alarm and thoughts of fear—but all settled in one thought: *how He loves and welcomes the poor and desolate*"—nor was her ever-present awareness of the sacred bond of Christian union forgotten—"He said, while the soul was preparing: 'See the Blood I shed for you, is at this very hour invoked upon you by your brother' [Bruté himself at the altar]."[38] And again, "Watching night and cramped breast made heavy head for Communion. As the tabernacle door opened— the pressing thought: This Bread *should not be given to a dog, Lord!* Immediately, as the eyes closed, a white old shepherd dog, feeding from the shepherd's hand in the midst of the flock, as I have seen in the fields between Pisa and Florence, came before me. Yes, my Savior, You feed your poor dog, who, at the first sight, can hardly be distinguished from the sheep—but the canine qualities You see!"[39]

In these two abject admissions of unworthiness the saint seems to express yet another insight into the "poor" for whom Jesus came, that even His holiest disciples rightly count themselves poor in order to attract His loving gaze and have His saving gospel preached to them. With her extraordinary talent for relating familiar objects to the divine truths they truly touched, Elizabeth glorified the house chapel's common little tabernacle by putting into simple words the awesome things that went on within it and urging Sisters and children alike to join actively in the sacred mysteries: "We who possess the actual presence of Our Lord in the Blessed Sacrament", she counseled, "should unite our homages to those which He offers day and night to His Father from our tabernacle in His quality of *victim* and intercessor."[40] And she gave a delightful turn to the narrative of the Last Supper: " 'The disciple whom Jesus loved'—and 'who leaned on His breast at supper'—we—not on His breast, but He on ours, indeed."[41] Nor was she unaware that this disciple was the same John who represented all God's sons and daughters when Jesus gave them into the keeping of His Mother.

Elizabeth's intimacy with the divine Guest in the Sacrament grew so that it easily tolerated the weakness of human nature and even more of illness, and she confessed to Bruté without the slightest compunction, in the wake of her brush with death in 1818, that "I went to sleep before I made any thanksgiving but *Te Deum* and *Magnificat* after Communion."[42] It was an intimacy shared by St. Thérèse of Lisieux, who refused to worry when she, too, would fall asleep after Communion, because, she reasoned, God loved her as much when she was asleep as when she was awake.

No matter the "alarm and thoughts of fear" that sometimes preceded her Communions, Elizabeth experienced the solace of the Eucharist to the full. "[If] as [is] certainly true . . . that bread naturally taken removes my hunger," she declared, "so this Heavenly Bread of Angels removes my pains, my cares—warms, cheers, soothes, contents and renews my whole being!"[43] Not alone a therapy of the soul but a therapy of the whole personality, healing physical sickness, banishing worry, bringing peace and contentment of mind. With what gladness, then, she clung to this solace through every twenty-four hours, without losing her awe of it: "I sit or stand opposite His tabernacle all day"—her room adjoined the chapel—"and keep the heart to it as the needle to the pole, and at night still more, even to folly; since I have so little right to be so *near* to Him."[44] (The writer has never forgotten the same awe and humility in an old religious who, recounting a trip in a car with a priest carrying Communion to the sick, said in wonder—she who had lived a busy and sophisticated life of service in high administrative positions—"Father, I rode in the same car with the *Blessed Sacrament!*")

For all her faith in the Eucharist, the ecstasies of her Communions, Elizabeth never forgot the responsibility and ultimate accounting that went with so unbelievably intimate a gift. She did not hesitate to state both with uncompromising bluntness, even to her innocent pupils on the eve of their first Communion: "I see you all around—at the foot of this tabernacle where the love of Our Jesus has so long waited for many of you", she said fondly, "but also I see the awful and dreadful account in His judgment of the use of this grace. My dearest girls, if you should—even one of you—be so unhappy as to abuse it—but I rather hope every heart is in earnest—you know already when it was prepared for you, when it was merited for each soul in particular."[45] It is not hard to detect the mother's anxiety yet also the mother's hope and trust.

Perhaps the crown of St. Elizabeth Ann's countless fervent Communions in a fervent life was one of her last, just three months before her holy death. Confined to bed by her infirmities, she lay there day by day waiting for each new meeting with her Lord. On the night of October 5–6, 1820, she fought a raging thirst throughout a wakeful night, refusing steadfastly the glass of water that would bring her relief, so that she might receive Communion in the morning (there were few concessions to the ill in the fasting regulations of those days). When, at last, Father Bruté entered her room, he recounted,

> Her joy was so uncommon that when I approached, and as I placed the ciborium upon the little table, she burst into tears, and, sobbing aloud, covered her face with her two hands. I thought first it was some fear of sin and, approaching her, I asked, "Be still, Mother! Peace, peace be to you! Here is the Lord of Peace! Have you any pain? Do you wish to confess?"
>
> "No, no! Only give Him to me!" . . . she said with an ardor, a kind of exclamation, and her whole face so inflamed that I was much affected.[46]

Here were the love and longing of a lifetime. They were surely fresh in Bruté's memory when he wrote, months later: "Will I ever forget that face, fired with love, melted in tears at His approach in Communion? To the last, exhausted death on that face—it was still inflamed, and blushed in ardent love, desire inexpressible of eternal union in Him."[47]

The remembrance of such communions was the cause of his reproaches on a spring evening after Elizabeth's death: "My Mother, O my Mother! What remembrance this evening of your fervent communions—why did I check your sobs, tears, almost cries, your whole countenance so inflamed—oh, why? I almost reproach it to my soul this evening—why not transports when *such* is our faith?—Our Jesus present and received!" The next thought was logical for a priest as holy as Bruté: "O faith! And I the priest every day at the altar! Where is mine, my Lord? Do give me the faith of that woman to whom—me seems—coming to her, entering her heart you said well pleased, 'O mulier, magna est fides tua!' "[48]

St. Elizabeth Ann first came to know Mary, the Mother of God, while she was sheltered with the Filicchis in Livorno. She tells of it artlessly in a diary intended for Rebecca Seton:

> A little prayer-book of Mrs. F[ilicchi]'s was on the table, and I opened [to] a little prayer of St. Bernard to the Blessed Virgin, begging her to be *our Mother;* and I said to her, with such a certainty that God would surely refuse nothing to *His Mother,* and that she could not help loving and pitying the poor souls he died for, that I felt really I had a Mother—which you know my foolish heart so often lamented to have lost in early days. From the first remembrance of infancy I have looked, in all the plays of childhood and wildness of youth, to the clouds for my mother; and at that moment it seemed as if I had found more than her, even in tenderness and pity of a mother. So I cried myself to sleep on her heart.[49]

These are extraordinary words from a woman who, as a devout adherent of the Protestant Episcopal Church, had just days or weeks before no concept of Mary as either universal Mother or Mediatrix. It is true that her grief for her husband, her loneliness and her deep maternal instinct made her especially receptive to the good news of Mary, but her instant responsiveness and accurate grasp of Mary's role in redemption suggest an exceptional grace of major importance. Certainly Mary was to play a special role in her own conversion and perfection, as well as in the establishment and devotion of her religious community. There is, besides, an essential justice in the immediate and lasting rapport between the heavenly Mother and Patroness of the Church in America and the woman who was in so many ways its Mother on earth.

It was this bond of motherhood that helped Elizabeth comprehend the Compassion of Mary, her role as Co-Redemptrix, even before it had been taught to her. As she stood before a masterwork in Florence, "A picture of the Descent from the Cross, nearly as large as life, engaged *my whole soul*—Mary at the foot of it expressed well that the iron had entered into hers, and the shades of death over her agonized countenance so strongly contrasted the heavenly peace of the dear Redeemer that it seems as if His pains had fallen on her. How hard it was to leave that picture, and how often, even in the few hours' interval since I have seen it, I shut my eyes and recall it in imagination!"[50] Unwittingly she had penetrated this sorrowful mystery as deeply as the same St. Bernard whose "little prayer" had introduced her to the Blessed Virgin. "Truly, O blessed Mother, a sword has pierced your heart", the great Father and Doctor had written.

> For only by passing through your heart could the sword enter the flesh of your Son. Indeed, after your Jesus—who belongs to everyone, but is especially yours—gave up His life, the cruel spear, which was not withheld from His lifeless body, tore open His side. Clearly, it did not touch His soul and could not harm Him, but it did pierce your heart. For surely His soul was no longer there, but yours could not be torn away. Thus the violence of sorrow has cut through your heart, and we rightly call you more than martyr, since the effect of compassion in you has gone beyond the endurance of physical suffering.

He went on to question why anyone should be "more surprised at the Compassion of Mary than at the passion of Mary's Son? For if He could die in body, could she not die with Him in spirit? He died in body through a love greater than anyone had known. She died in spirit through a love unlike any other since His."[51]

These two first contrasting embraces of Mary by St. Elizabeth Ann, in the relief of prayer and the starkness of crucifixion, are abundant proof that while Elizabeth's immediate acceptance of the Mother of God was warm and even impulsive in conformity with her nature, it was neither sentimental nor saccharine but was forged in the steel and sacrifice of that same nature.

The bond grew as Elizabeth returned to America and entered on her own long passion of religious uncertainty. "Anna coaxes me, when we are at our evening prayers, to say Hail Mary, and all say, '*Oh, do, Ma,* teach it to us!'" she told Amabilia Filicchi.

> Even little Bec tries to lisp it, though she can scarcely speak; and I ask my Savior why should we not say it. If anyone is in heaven, *His Mother* must be there. Are the angels, then, who are so often represented as being so interested for us on earth, more compassionate or more exalted than she is? Oh, no, no. Mary, our Mother, that cannot be. So I beg her with the tenderness and confidence of her child to pity us and guide us to the true faith, if we are not in it, and *if we are,* to obtain peace for my poor soul, that I may be a good mother to my poor darlings. For I know, if God should leave me to myself after all my sins, He would be justified; and since I read these books, my head is quite bewildered about the few who are saved. So I kiss her picture you gave me, and beg her to be a Mother to us.[52]

Despite Elizabeth's reliance on Mary, even this reliance eventually felt the suspicion of doubt as the clouds rolled thicker into her soul. "I fell on my face before God (remember I tell you all)", she confided to Antonio Filicchi in her agitation, "and appealed to Him as my righteous Judge, if hardness of heart, or unwillingness to be taught, or any human reasons, stood between me and the truth; if I would not rejoice to cast my sorrows in the bosom of the Blessed Mary . . . if once my soul could know it was pleasing to Him."[53] With what feelings of guilt she must have asked herself, "Could you believe that the prayers and litanies addressed to Our Blessed Lady"—she who had felt their solace—"were acceptable to God though not commanded in Scripture? . . ."[54] If only she had realized that "Our Blessed Lady" was a telltale phrase, revealing how far she had progressed in Catholic belief. But, if the mediation of Mary had been held up to question, however reluctantly, Elizabeth joyfully acknowledged its power in the crucial Sunday of mid-January 1805, which turned her firmly to the true Faith. "I became half crazy", she recalled for Amabilia, "and for the first time could not bear the sweet caresses of the darlings or bless their little dinner. O my God, that day! But it finished calmly at last—abandoning all to God—and a renewed confidence in the Blessed Virgin, whose mild and peaceful look reproached my bold excesses and reminded me to fix my mind above with better hopes."[55]

Years later, in the comfortable familiarity of settled faith, Elizabeth turned with perfect naturalness to the Sorrowful Mother as she nursed her dying Annina. On the feast of Mary's Purification she found herself "at the feet of our sweet, happy Mother Mary, listening to dear old Simeon doting on the darling Babe—offering the precious sufferer in my arms when He entered our chamber—and oh, to hold them both up to the Eternal Father! The child offering the mother, the mother the child. The sweet half-hour of love and peace with Jesus between us, as she sits on her bed of pain and I kneel beside her."[56] Surely she did not forget that it was Simeon who had prophesied the sword that was to tear the Virgin Mother's heart, or the awesome picture of the Descent from the Cross that had "engaged [her] whole soul" in Florence. The moving words of offering and sacrifice attest that she had entered into the Compassion of Mary. When Annina had gone, she continued to identify with that other Sorrowful Mother, "begging, crying to Mary to behold her Son and plead for us, and to Jesus to behold His Mother—to pity a Mother, a poor, poor Mother so uncertain of reunion".[57] The poignancy of the prayer and her trust are not lessened but given an agonized strength by the forlorn confession—made in honest humbleness or despairing grief—that darkness and uncertainty had engulfed her soul. *My God, My God, why have You forsaken Me?*

The maternity that united the Virgin Mary with Elizabeth

Seton is especially strong in an exquisite meditation for the feast of the Assumption. "Jesus nine months in Mary, feeding on her blood—Oh, Mary! These nine months", Elizabeth wrote in remembrance of a like joy she herself had known in carrying her children. Now she was savoring it again in transcendent communion with the divine motherhood. "Jesus on the breast of Mary, feeding on her milk! How long she must have delayed the weaning of such a child!!!! The infancy of Jesus—in her lap—on her knees as on His throne, while the rolling earth, within its sphere, adorned with mountains, trees and flowers is the throne of Mary and her Blessed Infant, caressing, playing in her arms. O Mary, how weak these words!" They were not weak in the remembrance of a mother's fondling and dandling her children—she had still the embraces and kisses of her growing brood—but they were weak in her groping to express the mystical endearments of that other Mother and her divine Child that Elizabeth was privileged to experience in her soul. "The youth, the obscure life, the public life of Jesus. Mary always, everywhere, in every moment, day and night, conscious she was His Mother!" As she had once used her little Catherine's childish interplays with herself as models for her own relationship with God, she now called upon her love for and pride in her children to help her comprehend the divine Motherhood and Sonship, grace building on nature. "Oh, glorious, happy Mother, even through the sufferings and ignominies of her Son." How well experience had taught her that true happiness was impervious to suffering. Then, the awe, the delight in the maternal perfection that she could only strive to emulate as best she could: "Her full conformity to Him—O virtues of Mary—the constant delight of the Blessed Trinity—she alone giving Them more glory than all heaven together. Mother of God! Mary! Oh, the purity of Mary! The humility, patience, love, of Mary!—to imitate at humblest distance."[58]

Elizabeth's exquisite ending to her Assumption meditation was at the same time theological and illumined: "How happy the earth to possess her so long—a secret blessing to the rising Church—the Blessed Trinity could not part so soon with the perfect praise arising from the Earth as long as she remained—how darkened in the sight of angels when she was removed from it."[59]

Elizabeth also pursued her mother's intuitions of Mary with her Sisters, as an outline for a conference attests. "We honor her continually with Our Jesus", she told them. "His nine months within her"—the thought inspired a fresh spate of spiritual insights—"what passed between them—she alone knowing Him"—there was indeed a time when Mary alone of all mankind knew that the Messiah had come—"He her only tabernacle.... Mary, *full of grace, Mother of Jesus!* Oh, we love and honor Our Jesus when we love and honor her"—how plain this truth was to her now that she was free of the cultural bonds of her religious upbringing—"a true proof of our blessed Church being the one Jesus best loves". She finished with an abrupt transition, to bring the holy Mother into the very hearts of the Sisters: "Mary, the first Sister of Charity on earth".[60] It was, indeed, and is, something for them to ponder.

The saint shared her delighted contemplation of the love of Jesus and Mary as He lay hidden in her chaste womb with St. Louise de Marillac, foundress with St. Vincent de Paul of the Daughters of Charity, whose Rule and spirit Elizabeth had chosen for her own community and who was like Elizabeth a widow and mother. It was an established devotion of both, nurtured by their motherhood, as Elizabeth bore witness in a note to Bruté, perhaps at Christmastime: "Blessed, it would please your so kind heart to know that this week past or more, our soul's dear Baby has been much more present to me than the beloved babes of former days, when I carried and suckled them. He, the Jesus Babe, so unspeakably near and close, hugged by His poor, silently delighted wild one!"[61]

As Elizabeth's knowledge of holy things deepened daily, and her love for them took more total possession of her mind and heart, the place of Mary in the divine plan and consequently her place in every part of it became all the closer to Elizabeth. Acknowledging Mary as Mediatrix, "returning our love to JESUS for us, our prayer passing through her heart with reflected love and excellence, Jesus delighted to receive our love embellished and purified through the heart of Mary, as from the heart of a FRIEND, everything delights us"—she finishes by asking in happy abandonment, "How can we honor the mysteries of Our Jesus without honoring Mary in them all—how unhappy they who deprive themselves of such happiness." She now saw Mary everywhere in God, as she indeed is: "Jesus in Mary, Mary in Jesus in our prayers—her name so often in the divine sacrifice."[62]

Elizabeth never gave herself to sleep, that prophetic sister of death, without "my crucifix under my pillow and the Blessed Virgin's picture pressed on the heart", and she once described for her sister Mary Post how she clung to them during a frightful storm that seemed to her a warning of death and judgment:

Think of the contrast, to wake with the sharpest lightnings and loudest thunder succeeding each other so rapidly that they seemed to stop but half a moment between, to give time for a sense of the danger. Every part of the house seemed struck in an instant, and the roarings of the winds and torrents through the mountains so impetuous, that it seemed they must destroy, if the lightnings should spare.

Our God, what a moment! I had no power to rise, or to remember I was a sinner, or give a thought to the horrors of death, or the safety of the children. God my Father in that moment so pressing—and the plunge in eternity the next instant.

O my Mary! How tight I held my little picture as a mark of confidence in her prayers who must be tenderly interested for souls so dearly purchased by her Son, and the crucifix held up as a silent prayer which offered all His merits and sufferings as our only hope—How you laugh at your poor, half-brained Betsey Seton, but never mind—The decadence of the storm brought me down from the clouds, and I felt really, I suppose, as one who is drawn back from the door of eternity, after having been half in, and I crept away to the choir window to see what had become of my little, peaceable Queen, who was wrapped in clouds alternately lightened as they passed over her with so much brightness, they appeared at first sight like balls of light hastening towards us, while she was tak[ing] her quiet course above them, to disappear behind the mountain.

There again I found the soul which fastens on God. Storms or whirlwinds pass by or over it, but cannot stop it one moment. My Mary, dear, how nice it would have been to have died then—if it had been the right time. But since it was not, here I am, very happy to meet all the countenances of terror and wonder this morning, and the repeated appeal of: "O Mother, what a night!"[63]

When, a few years later, "the right time" had come, Elizabeth knew only the happy contentment all those nights with the "crucifix under my pillow and the Blessed Virgin's picture pressed on the heart" had earned. "If this be the way of death, nothing can be more peaceful and happy," she said one day, chatting with Sister Cecilia O'Conway, "and if I am to recover, still how sweet to rest in the arms of Our Lord!" Peace and happiness and the absence of all fear were not the only rewards prepared for her who had loved her Lord and His Blessed Mother so dearly and faithfully. "It seems as if Our Lord stood continuously by me in a corporeal form to comfort, cheer and encourage me in the different weary and tedious hours of pain", she went on, and her words are not to be taken lightly. "Sometimes sweet Mary, also, gently coaxing me—but you will laugh at my imagination."[64] Sister Cecilia did not laugh. Nor did anyone else. Elizabeth's assistant, Sister Xavier, testified of her blessed death: "I do not know if you will give . . . the name of superstition to that which I felt at this moment. It seemed to me that Our Lord was there, near to her, very close, awaiting this good soul."[65]

6

"IF YOU WOULD BE MY DISCIPLE . . ."

One of the mysteries of today's contrary world is the silent disappearance of the words *penance* and *mortification* from the Christian and even the religious vocabulary. There is much talk of self-fulfillment, little of self-discipline; much talk of attaining human justice, little of satisfying divine justice. Yet penance and mortification have been urged as instruments of self-purification, perfection and salvation by ascetical masters from earliest Christian times, indeed, since Jesus Christ Himself insisted, "Whoever wishes to be my follower must deny his very self, take up his cross each day and follow in my steps."[1]

Elizabeth Seton understood from the beginning the necessity of taking up her cross and did so willingly. She learned early that the cross was the mark and abiding providence of Christians. Thus she wrote in her *Journal* on the eve of her father's last illness and death: "The cup which Our Father has given us, shall we not drink it? Blessed Savior, by the bitterness of Thy pains we may estimate the force of Thy love. We are *sure* of Thy kindness and compassion. Thou wouldst not willingly call on us to suffer. Thou hast declared unto us that all things shall work together for our good, if we are faithful to Thee. Therefore, if Thou so ordainst it: welcome, disappointments and poverty; welcome, sickness and pain; welcome, even shame and contempt and calumny!" She left out nothing. Nor was she speaking from an ivory tower of lofty sentiments, safe from the harsh realities she welcomed. She had already suffered them all with her husband in his financial disaster and bankruptcy. Nor was it superhuman stoicism, however admirable, but earnest, humble recognition of the Christian way. "If this be a rough and thorny path, it is the one which Thou hast gone before us. Where we see Thy footsteps, we cannot repine." And her confidence was sure and unafraid. "Meanwhile, Thou wilt support us with the consolations of Thy grace; even here Thou canst compensate us for any temporal sufferings by the possession of that peace which the world can neither give nor take away."[2]

Elizabeth understood, too, that "temporal sufferings" were most often caused by fellow creatures, by-products of the daily give-and-take of imperfect beings with wounded natures, and sought to offset their harm by striving "not in any instance or by any provocation to retaliate anger or passion—to speak harshly or severely, *even if the truth,* of any fellow creature, in all difficulties and situations contrary to the bent of my inclination to *remember my cross* and for what purpose I wear it—in the name of my Savior and in firm reliance and trust in *His* assistance."[3] The cross she referred to was a gift from her father, and she loved it as "the mark of my Captain and Master whom I was to follow so valiantly".[4] Most significant was her use of it as a reminder that she was to imitate her Lord in meeting trials, but especially in doing violence to herself and abandoning all out of love, as He did.

Elizabeth understood well the reason. She was as imperfect, her nature as wounded, as her nearest neighbor's, and from the realization came that honest sense of sin that is essential to common goodness, to say nothing of the holiness Elizabeth Seton was to attain. On an August afternoon in 1802 she put it in words: "Solemnly in the presence of my Judge—I resolve *through His grace*—to remember my *infirmity* and my *sin*—to keep the door of my lips—to consider the causes of sorrow for sin in *myself* and *them* whose souls are as dear to me as my own."[*][5]

---

[*] It is obvious from the date that it was all part of the practical working out of the covenant made with her Lord the preceding May, and the reference to loved ones indicates, even in something so intimate as blame, that apostleship was always part of anything she did.

The saint, like all saints, never lost the sense of sin. Indeed, the more she pondered it in her mature spiritual years, the sharper it became and the more she was able to probe its depths. Thus she came to the terrible truth that "when we sin, we not only sin in the presence of God, *but in God Himself;* for since He is the source of motion and life, it follows that the sinner uses the concurrence of God Himself to offend and sin against Him, turning the means of life, health, time, etc., *powers of nature and grace,* to this horrid perversion and abuse against this Almighty Giver"—and she finished thoughtfully, "which explains to us in some degree the eternity of Hell torments".[6]

The practice of living habitually in God's Presence helped refine the sense of sin, Elizabeth discovered, for "all things work *together* unto good. A soul faithful to this holy exercise becomes so timorous and tender towards God", she told her Sisters, "that the least fault it commits is a pain to it, the smallest wound of conscience a torment, till it has humbled itself before Him and had recourse to His infinite mercies." A *real* turning to God in sorrow, she cautioned, "not like those who are restless till they go to confession, and afterwards are neither better or more humble"— she was a shrewd judge of souls—no, that kind of restlessness had nothing to do with the honest emotions of regret that were perfectly natural in the circumstances. "Far from suffering our faults and imperfections to turn us from the presence of God through the uneasiness and chagrin they cause us," she continued reassuringly, "we should return to it as quickly as a little child to its mother after it has had a fall by letting go her hand, and hold to that dear hand with new care and fidelity." The soul practiced in seeking God after some momentary lapse of attention, or even of strayed loyalty, will become so wonderfully used to being with God that nothing can take His place, like Mary Magdalen, who "at the Sepulchre was not dazzled or stopt by the beauty of the angels there, but went on seeking her God and could find no rest but in Him"; in the same way, "a heart which loses God, truly will stop at nothing created, because nothing can supply for its God, which it seeks everywhere and in all things".[7]

When young Cecilia Seton had been drawn by Elizabeth's example of Christian devotion and practice to emulate her, the older woman—now more than her friend but de facto her mother, since William Seton had at his father's death taken all his young brothers and sisters into his own home—cautioned her, "If you find that there are any obstacles in your way—and doubtless you will find many, as every Christian does in the fulfillment of their duty—still persevere with yet more earnestness, and rejoice to bear your share in the *Cross,* which is our passport and seal to the Kingdom of our Redeemer."[8]

Elizabeth gave only advice she herself followed. In the agony of the *lazaretto* she wrote, "Not only willing to take my cross, but kissed it, too."[9]

The difficulty of Elizabeth's submission is revealed in a flare of passion when the long imprisonment was almost over. Talking in thought to the absent captain of the quarantine, she scolded: "The dampness about us would be thought dangerous for a person in health—and my William's sufferings—oh! Well I know that God is *above, Capitano,* you need not always point your silent look and finger there; if I thought our condition the providence of *man,* instead of the 'weeping Magdalen'—as you so graciously call me— you would find me a lioness, willing to burn your *lazaretto* about your ears, if it was possible, that I might carry off my poor prisoner to breathe the air of heaven in some more seasonable place."[10] The pain of submission is equally evident in a poignant passage written for her eyes alone, days before the death of Rebecca Seton:

> The dear, faithful, tender friend of my soul through every varied scene of many years of trial, gone—only the shadow remaining, and that in a few days must pass away! The home of plenty and comfort, the society of sisters united by prayers and divine affections, the evening hymns, the daily readings, the sunset contemplations, the service of holy days together, the kiss of peace, the widows' visits—all, all gone forever! And is poverty and sorrow the only exchange? My husband, my sisters, my home, my comforts—poverty and sorrow. Well, with God's blessing, you, too, shall be changed into dearest friends.[11]

Unlettered as yet in asceticism, Elizabeth was nevertheless affirming in word and deed that life lived in conformity to God's Will is a mortification. Certainly hers had been. That she did not realize that her constant, willing acceptance of it had already had its effect on her soul was a grace. She never gloried in the hardships of her life but only in the Cross of Our Lord Jesus Christ.

Nor did Elizabeth complain. Her love for God had made her the complete realist in matters spiritual and temporal. When she told Julia Scott, "God has given me a great deal to do",[12] she was stating a simple fact. When she told her, " 'I rise up early and late take rest,' you may be sure. Never before after twelve, and oftener one. Such is the allotment", she was stating a simple fact. That she added, "And as everybody has their *pride* of some sort, I cannot deny that this is mine",[13] she was not boasting, only acknowledging her artless satisfaction in doing what was expected of her. The truest assessment of her daily life and attitude was in the vignette of one of her days: "I have cut out my two *suits* today and partly made one. Heard all the lessons, too, and had a two hours' visit from my widow Veley—no work, no wood, child sick, etc.—and should I complain, with a bright fire within, bright, bright *moon* over my shoulder, and the darlings all well, hallooing and dancing?—I have played for them this half hour."[14] A classic example of "count your blessings", but raised—the piety of her life bears witness to it—to the plane of true mortification and prayer.

With this love of the Cross long Elizabeth's only way of life, she pounced with delight on a new revelation of its power in her Catholic friends of Livorno. "Why, Rebecca," she wrote in wonderment,

> they believe all we do and suffer—if we offer it for our sins— serves to expiate them. You may remember when I asked Mr. H[obart] what was meant by fasting in our prayer book—as I found myself on Ash Wednesday morning saying so foolishly to God, "I turn to you in fasting, weeping, and mourning," and I had come to church with a hearty breakfast of buckwheat

cakes and coffee, and full of life and spirits, with little thought of my sins—you may remember what he said about its being old customs, etc. Well the dear Mrs. F[ilicchi], who I am with, never eats, this season of Lent, till after the clock strikes three. Then the family assembles. And she says she offers her weakness and pain of fasting for her sins, united with Our Savior's sufferings. I like that very much.[15]

I like that very much—a startling sentiment, humanwise, in one who had just suffered the draining trial of the *lazaretto* and who might be expected to flee from even the thought of pain, for the human frame naturally shrinks from it, but sure proof that Elizabeth Seton was not accustomed to wasting her pain, indeed, that she had penetrated the mysterious relationship of sin and suffering, and sure proof, further, that the soil of her soul lay fertile for the great tree of faith the Lord had ready for it. *A humble and contrite heart, O Lord, you will not spurn.*

Sin and its punishment were very much in Elizabeth's thoughts at the time. On the voyage to Italy she had set Anna crying by telling her that "*we offended God every day*", and had herself, in a kind of Calvinist terror, penned a desperate resolution. "Considering the *infirmity* and corrupt nature which would overpower the spirit of grace", she had reasoned,

and the enormity of the offense to which the least indulgence of them would lead me—in the anguish of my soul, shuddering to offend my adored Lord, I have this day solemnly engaged that, through the strength of His Holy Spirit, I will not again expose that corrupt and infirm nature to the smallest temptation I can avoid; and, therefore, if my Heavenly Father will once more *reunite us all,* that I will make a daily sacrifice of every *wish,* even the *most innocent,* lest they should betray me to the deviation from the solemn and sacred vow I have now made.[16]

The extravagance of the bargain betrays Elizabeth's depression and desperation, but there is no mistaking the clear vision and determination. On the voyage home, with the opening of her spiritual horizon in Italy, the vision was even clearer, and she cried out in a fright inspired by the sight of Nelson's warships off Trafalgar, "Oh, my God, if I should die in the midst of so much sin and so little penitence! how terrible it will be to fall into Thy hands!"[17]

The sense of sin, thus, still brought Elizabeth terror, but her own seasoned love of God and the new revelation of it learned from her devout Catholic friends would soon begin to change things. In the fresh crucible of troubles, she might tell Antonio, "Our God is pleased to hammer me like a truly poor sinner"[18]— but she was about to put aside any religion of fear. Symbolic of the happy change was her description of her first confession: "So delighted now to prepare for this good confession which, bad as I am, I would be ready to make on the house top to insure the good *absolution* I hope for after it."[19] Her eagerness for what to many converts is an object of fear was rooted in a deep longing for an authentic forgiveness of her sins. Two months before, she had described her despair of it in her last attendance at a Protestant service: "At the bowing of my heart before the Bishop to receive his absolution—which is given publicly and universally to all in the church—I had not the least faith in his prayer, and looked for an apostolic loosing from my sins, which by the books Mr. H[obart] had given me to read, I find they do not claim or admit."[20] As Elizabeth prepared now for that apostolic fiat, she looked forward to setting "out [on] a new life, a new existence itself. No great difficulty for me to be ready for it, for truly my life has been well culled over in bitterness of soul, these months of sorrow past." Then: "It is done! Easy enough . . . oh, Amabilia, how awful those words of unloosing after thirty years' bondage! I felt as if my chains fell, as those of St. Peter at the touch of the divine Messenger. My God, what new scenes for my soul!"[21]

Elizabeth did not, however, in her newfound innocence forget the lesson of satisfaction for sin she had learned in Livorno, as she confided to Amabilia: "Much he [Antonio] says of my bringing all the children to your Gubbio to find peace and abundance. But I have a long life of sins to expiate."[22] She was still conscious of the debt years later, in remonstrating with her son William for his silence: "February your last date, and here 25th July. Eyes fill and heart aches; but God is God, and the hardest penance I can pay in this life is separation from you, and I must bear it. Oh, if but at last to be *united forever!*"[23]

Nor did Elizabeth fail to teach the lesson to her daughter Annina, who, though her sins were scarcely "as scarlet", yet freely offered a most painful expiation for them. Gasping for breath on her mother's knees the night before she died, the young girl scribbled this moving Act of Consecration:

> Amiable and Adorable Savior, at the foot of Your cross I come to consecrate myself to You forever. . . . O dear Jesus, I offer Thee all my sufferings, little as they are now, and willingly accept with resignation—oh, by Thy grace let me say with love!—whatever You will please to send me in future. I offer in union with Your blessed merits all the sufferings I ever suffered: those which I endured at a time I did not know how to unite them to Yours, those I have experienced during this last sickness— I offer more particularly to Your glory, and in expiation of the offenses and grievous sins committed during my life. O my Jesus, pardon the impatiences, ill humors and numberless other faults.[24]

The love of the Cross, which Elizabeth found at every turning, remained a constant in her soul. She was sometimes awkward in accepting it, perhaps because it presented itself in the most surprising places. For example, when she had lost for a time a roof over her head and food for her children and was obliged to take refuge with her sister Mary Post, pride and the natural tension between siblings obscured the Cross. "My sister procures fish with so great expense and difficulty (really as if for the greatest stranger!)", she complained to Antonio, "that my bread-and-water spirit is ashamed to partake of it."[25] And again: "Some proposals have been made me of keeping a *tea* store or china shop, or small school for *little* children (too young, I suppose, to be taught the 'Hail Mary'). In short, Tonino, they do not know what to do with me, *but God does;* and when His blessed time is come, we shall know."[26]

Despite her all-too-human indignation, the apprehension of God and His ways was not lost, and she begged Antonio not to give her "the scolding I know I deserve".[27] Her friend Eliza Sadler, however, did not spare her. "Do your sister and her husband really desire your remaining with them?" she asked.

> Of this there can be little doubt, however some inequalities of temper may seem to contradict it. . . . Perhaps not even *I* have it in my power to conceive how hard (in your situation) such inequalities are to submit to. But let us only repeat . . . that the harder they are to bear, the greater will be your reward if you bear them as a cross at the foot of which feelings of worldly considerations must be sacrificed when we resolve to do all for the glory of God. Now this can only be done from a conviction that your duty is to remain where you are, or rather that you are placed there by the divine Will."[28]

Elizabeth confessed the understandable truth to Julia Scott: "It seemed as if there was no escape from the inconveniences and trouble I was necessitated to give the family of my brother P[ost]. The more kind they were to me, the more painful was my sense of it."[29] As might be expected of a soul normally equable, Elizabeth's soon recovered its balance. "The rubs, etc., are all past", she assured Julia. "No one appears to know it except by showing redoubled kindness — *only* a few knotty hearts that must talk of something, and the worse they say is: 'So much trouble has turned her brain.' Well, I kiss my crucifix, which I have loved for so many years, and say they are only mistaken."[30]

Elizabeth had rightly professed in the same letter, "I am gently, quietly and silently a good Catholic."[31] She had become so in large measure through the sensible, steady direction of Father Jean Tisserant, who had discerned the basic docility of her soul and relied upon it. For example: "You tell me you were prevented from going to church on Ash Wednesday. . . . Your Lent has commenced with a sacrifice and with the mortification of the will, and with good resolutions which I hope God will bless. Strengthen them by the practice of what the Church enjoins at this holy time. But do not exaggerate things. Remember what you have to do as a mother, and in the employment which you have undertaken."[32]

The surprise of the Cross came again, even in the first days of Elizabeth's joy of having attained her dream of the religious life, with the petulant leave-taking of Dubourg and the arrogance of his successor, David. Her own inclination was to avoid conflict, but conscience told her what she had to do, to defend her community. "Circumstances have all so combined as to create in my mind a confusion and want of confidence in my superior which is indescribable", she wrote desperately to Archbishop Carroll. "If my own happiness was only in question, I should say: 'How good is the cross for me; this is my opportunity to ground myself in patience and perseverance': and *my reluctance to speak* on a subject which I know will give you uneasiness is so great that I would certainly be silent. But as the good Our Almighty God may intend to do by means of this community may be very much impeded . . . it is absolutely necessary."[33] The distinction between personal concerns and the common good and the consequent responsibilities were clear in her mind, as well as the personal suffering demanded.

Carroll, as the representative of Christ and His Church, responded by making this very point while at the same time sanctifying Elizabeth's suffering by identifying it positively as her way of the cross. "The proposal, if renewed, will not create any uneasiness on your account", he said confidently—the crisis had now reached the point where David actually considered removing the foundress from office—

> You have gone through many trials in overcoming the obstructions, interior and exterior, which were interposed to your change of religion. To these, other difficulties equally or more painful succeeded; but it has still pleased God to reserve another which must naturally disappoint your expectations more than any preceding one. That is, you are destined to be tried by disapprobation and humiliation, where you expected to meet confidence and tranquility. This was wanting, perhaps, to per-

fect your other sacrifices, and to operate in your heart a perfect disengagement from human things and expectations—even the consolations of religious retirement.[34]

Elizabeth took the proferred cross to her heart and with it not only the exterior assaults on her and her Sisterhood which would pass in time but also the day-to-day demands on her as its Mother, which would not. "I am at peace", she told Eliza Sadler, just days after receipt of the Archbishop's letter.

> A lazy, sleepy soul, give me but quiet, and all is given; yet that quiet is in the midst of fifty children all day, except the early part of morning and a part of the afternoon. But *quiet it is.* Order and regularity cannot be skipped over here, and I am in the full possession of that principle which in the world passed either for hypocrisy or a species of it. You know, that manner of looking upon twenty people in the room with a look of affection and interest, showing an interest for all and a concern in all of their concerns.

She went on to draw the picture of her straitened day with her usual vividness: "You know I am a mother encompassed by many children of different dispositions, not all equally amiable or congenial; but bound to love, instruct and provide for the happiness of all, to give the example of cheerfulness, peace, resignation, and consider individuals more as proceeding from the same origin and tending to the same end than in the different shades of merit and demerit."[35]

The common life is indeed the greatest mortification, as St. John Berchmans learned in his short, youthful experience of it. The most committed community is made up, after all, of men with fallen natures, all obliged by their acceptance of the Rule to live in inescapable intimacy. In such a way of life, the smallest eccentricity of the one becomes the most insufferable irritant to the other. The Little Flower confessed that a companion in the laundry splashed her with water to the point of utter distraction. But the common life is especially difficult for the superior who, because of the evenhandedness and example demanded by the office, is constrained more than others in word and act.

Elizabeth's courage in taking up the cross unceasingly for the good of the community was a model for her Sisters, and she must have had a just pride in their imitation of it, for example, when they willingly accepted the hardships of their first mission outside the Valley during the turmoil of the War of 1812. The community *Minutes* record their valor:

> A letter was read from the Archbishop which seemed for a moment to raise obstacles to the Sisters taking charge of the orphan establishment—yet leaving it in our power to decide. These obstacles only presenting personal inconveniences, the Sisters generously determined to meet them and begin the good work. Another letter to the same purport was read from the Vicar General and one from Reverend Mr. Hurley [both of Philadelphia], the present menacing aspect of public affairs rendering it dangerous and disagreeable to the Sisters—unanimously agreed that no personal inconvenience should prevent Sisters of Charity doing what duty and charity required.[36]

The measure of the heroicity of these young nuns was in their use of the word *inconveniences* to describe the dangers and trials they were to face.

The mission's first Sister Servant, Rose White, wrote with simplicity of the deprivations of the first year: "The Asylum was in debt five thousand dollars, the subscriptions for its support few; the embargo made goods double price, and it was often told us to reflect that the sum allowed for support was only six hundred dollars a year. They had no occasion to remind us, for our fears were so great that we would not be able to make out that for three months we never eat bread at dinner, but used potatoes; no sugar in our coffee, which was made of corn." Even the orphans suffered. "The poor children had not been accustomed to get any sugar in their nursery beverage which was weak coffee and dry bread, sugar being very high. However, Rev. Mr. Hurley, hearing of our not using sugar, commanded us to use it, and some was sent."[37] There can be little doubt that the appalling mortifications forced on these pioneer Sisters in their utter poverty and hard lives earned the success and spread of the Sisters of Charity of St. Joseph's. The sufferings of the little innocents did their part, too!

Elizabeth did not hesitate to urge the cross on those she loved. "Look up!" she rallied her friend and benefactor George Weis. "The highest *there* were lowest *here*.... Now, my friend, we are in the true and sure way of salvation for that long, long eternity before us; if only we keep courage we will go to heaven on horseback instead of idling and creeping along.... George, George, be a man! but a supernatural man crucified in Christ."[38]

Lest Weis miss the depth of her meaning, Elizabeth drew graphic pictures of the bloody union the words "crucified in Christ" signified: "If we sink so soon in the day of trial, my friend, how will we be able to keep in the bloody footsteps of our Leader—oh, look upon Him, see His look of love and sorrow while He looks behind after you and calls, 'Come, follow Me'—Calvary is the rendezvous—Thus, my dear George, both you and I *must* meet Him—we must be crucified—it is in vain to start, or think of escaping."[39] And again: "As often as I look at the crucifix I think of You as if I could see Your name was written there on our crucified Lord, as indeed it is, my poor George."[40]

Elizabeth included herself in the exhortation, not only to encourage her suffering friend by her company but also because she was truly and completely united to him and his suffering. First of all by prayer: "Oh, that the Adored would give you a spark of the fire He has put in my heart since I bid you the last *A Dieu*," she wished aloud with childlike simplicity, "but I will use that fire to beg you may be supported or carried through this voyage of sorrow which has beset you."[41] Then, by full intention: "Happy would I be to take the sorrow and trouble of you all, if you might have the merit"[42]—here, indeed, was unselfish affection, spiritual affection even more telling than the giving of life—"Our Lord knows, my good friend, I would gladly give my life to do you any real good," she assured him, "but you know well what I think of the troubles of this life. I wish them even to be the portion and inheritance of my children, so how can I desire my poor friend to be without them."[43]

The wish for her children and all her loved ones to be burdened with the cross did not dispel Elizabeth's compassion for them. In fact, their suffering weighted down her own but at the same time increased the bond of their love, as she assured George Weis: "I know you suffer more for your dear wife than for yourself, which is the double trouble, poor friend, and you will have the double blessing, too, if you only persevere."[44] Most of all, however, to bear the sufferings of loved ones increased union with Jesus. "If Our Lord suffered us to bear our misery alone without affecting the dearest part of ourselves," she explained to Weis, "we would not suffer like Himself whose whole suffering was for us, and the injuries endured by His Eternal Father."[45]

Elizabeth was not so insensitive to weak human nature, either in herself or in others, as to forget the promised rewards of suffering. "Our cross will soon be taken off", she assured Weis, "look only forward to our long, long Eternity—Annina cries to all from her grave how quickly everything passes—my poor, poor George, take courage—sow in tears and reap in joy, look to the Master Carpenter you follow after[*]—I would be very sorry [if] He would divide our lot from His and treat us better than He did Himself."[46] And again she exclaimed, "That bright and glorious cross which we now drag along through the mud and dirt, how beautiful and lovely will it appear when we shall find it opens the door of our eternal happiness for us . . . remember, there is but one place of true rendezvous for true souls."[47]

Indeed, Elizabeth insisted, the rewards were often bestowed here and now, as if God could not wait to indulge those in whom He was well pleased. "Your troubles I find, like my own, are multiplied," she admitted to George, "and so will our comforts be when this dark night of life is over. . . . Won't we sing alleluias in the morning!—You may depend." Even now, although "I do not

[*] George Weis was a carpenter by trade.

grow *very* fat nor strong in the body—yet the soul is so well at liberty that everything except eternity seems but a dream, a tiresome dream—sometimes—at others it thirsts for pains and knows no pleasure but in suffering."[48]

Nonetheless, wherever the reward, Elizabeth loved her friend too dearly and rightly to wish his sufferings away. On the contrary: "I hope your cross may increase till it purifies you like pure gold," was all her comfort, "and woe to you (knowing as well as you do how rich a treasure you have) [if you] do not let it work its effect in you."[49]

Elizabeth could not forbear to season her uncompromising counsel with wit and teasing. She suggested that Weis tell a mutual friend "that we have adopted his motto: '*Well* enough to work, and bad enough to suffer'".[50] And she wondered whether "our little mischievous Cecil has procured you all these blessings for having so tenderly received and waited on her in her last days of exile*—indeed she is capable of all that spiritual malice could do, for you may depend, [she] would not be ungrateful."[51]

A truly remarkable memorial to St. Elizabeth Seton's love of the Cross of her Lord Jesus Christ is a unique meditation on "the communion of the cross", in which she contrasts and unites both infinite mysteries. "It is strictly true that altho' there is no possible advantage to be compared with the happiness of receiving Our Lord and Savior in the holy Eucharist, who is our very life in all our sufferings," she begins, "yet we also receive Him by the communion of His cross, that is to say, we may *unite with Him,* we *draw His spirit on us,* and it is very certain that we receive no grace in the communion of the holy Eucharist but in proportion as we receive it in the communion of *the cross.* We can know the value of neither, it is true, without Faith"—she continues, building her sacred analogy on the divine and indispensable common denominator of all religious belief and practice—"and as when we are called to participate at Our Lord's table we go joyfully, not stopping on what *we see,* but on what *we believe,* so when He

---

* Cecilia Seton died in George Weis' house in Baltimore.

invites us to come and receive Him in afflictions and sufferings, we should receive His chalice with the same ardor and *drink His Blood by Faith* without looking at the veils under which it is hidden"—in Elizabeth's day, of course, the holy Sacrament was received under only one species, the species of bread, which made easier the comparisons between receiving the Lord's Body in joy and His Blood (the communion of the Cross) in suffering; nevertheless—"Without this firm *Faith* we see nothing but a cross of *wood* in the *cross* of Our Lord, as we see nothing but *bread* in the Sacrament of His Body."

Certain aspects of the communion of the Cross are favorable to our weakened nature because they preclude mistaken self-interest and self-indulgence: "The great advantage of the communion of the cross is that we receive it when *Our Lord* Himself pleases and at the time He sees best . . . we may go to the table of Our Lord when He did not call us there, when He only bears with our presence, but we never receive Him in the communion of the cross without being called by Himself; it is a mandate from heaven itself we obey.

"We need not go to church to make this communion of suffering", she urges. "Our Savior comes to find us wherever we may be." Further, "angels can praise and love Him with us; this glory of suffering with and for our Head is for us alone as His happy members."

This was the center of all penitential argument and action, the Suffering Servant prophesied by Isaiah, the crucified Lord: "When Our Savior offers us His cross in any way, it is Himself, it is His own Blood He offers. . . . Approach, then, to participate it", she pleads, "and do not overturn the chalice on its altar . . . or lose one drop of the Precious Blood it contains in order to spare our own."

To spare our own! Elizabeth spoke now with the unerring eye of the saint and the sadness it brought:

Unhappily, we are apt to think the very least suffering is too much, because we are lovers with our lips rather than our heart, while a true lover of Christ can never have enough of His cross. . . . We open the door when He comes to us as the spouse in the canticles, crowned with lilies, but when He wears His garment of ignominy or His blood-stained robe of which the prophet speaks, we are struck with dread, and would be tempted to shut out our blessed *Spouse of Blood,* although He is covered with it but to save us. . . . This is because we love ourselves much more than we love Him.

Despite the sad truth, Elizabeth was too knowledgable and compassionate of human nature to leave it at that. "All He asks of us is our good will", she coaxes.

We are never strong enough to bear our cross, it is the cross which carries us, nor so weak as to be unable to bear it, since the weakest become strong by its virtue. . . . He is a Physician who pays His patient, and gives a great recompense for the smallest pains, tho' we owe these pains to His justice. . . . It is God alone we must look at in all that befalls us, small or great, and be persuaded that men and devils combined can do nothing ever so small but what He permits, and He permits no pain or trial whatever to befall us, but for the exercise of our VIRTUE and His glory.

In one sentence she encompasses this wondrous communion of the Cross, with the regret and the ardor it generates: "Our Lord, it is true, is content with our docility and resignation," she admits reluctantly, "but to this high mystery of our eternal union with Him we should bring the burning fire of love and gratitude."[52]

Elizabeth's lessons in mortification were turned back on her on one occasion when she admonished Annina—now doubly her child, since the girl had joined the Sisterhood—"for the little care of her health: rising at the first bell and being on the watch to ring it at the moment the clock struck, washing at the pump in the severest weather, eating what sickened her stomach—'Ah, dear Mother,' was the dying girl's reply, 'if Our Lord called me up to meditate, was I wrong to go? If I washed at the pump, did not others more delicate do it? If I ate what I did not like, was it not proper, since it was but a common Christian act to control my appetite?"[53] That the Mother recorded it in her *Spiritual Journal* is proof of her secret satisfaction.

When the last weeks of her own dying were upon her, the Mother, forgetting her remonstrances to her dying child, pursued with the wonderful perverse logic of the saints the same mortified path she had protested. The authority for this is no less than her spiritual director, Father Bruté. "She continued to follow as closely as possible the exercises and rules of the house, being assisted in doing so by a Sister who read and prayed with her", he told Antonio Filicchi.

> This she did until her death, with great fidelity and perseverance— manifested her uneasiness when some point of rule could not be fulfilled and supplying it as soon as there was an opportunity. Being obliged to make use of mitigations and necessary exemptions, she avoided them as much as she could without affectation. Sometimes she made excuses to her Sisters for what she termed her weakness, and she reproached herself for paying attention to it; and she endeavored as much as possible to repair what she considered a fault by mortifying herself the more. On one occasion she sent for me and lamented so earnestly, with tears that elicited mine, the relief she experienced and the comparative comfort she enjoyed in the use of a mattress that had been provided for Rebecca when she suffered too much to bear the hardness of the ordinary bed—and this mattress they had given to her.[54]

Elizabeth herself corroborated Bruté's testimony in the very last letter she wrote, which took her "near a day to write . . . blowing, puffing, all the time", to Sister Elizabeth Boyle, "dearest old partner of my cares and bearer of my burdens": "When I used to hear of their sending children's bills to Superior or paying out money, in the lowest moments when I could not turn on the pillow without hartshorn," she confessed, "I would stop them; for as Jane and I only had known, they were all in the dark. It soon pleased God I could answer and see to those things without letting them go out of their own old track."[55]

The inward mortification of the mind and will was supreme in Elizabeth Seton's practice and teaching. "You must be in right earnest, or you will do little or nothing", she told her Sisters with her usual energy.

What sort of interior life would you lead, if every time the door opens, or if any one passes you, you must look up; if you must hear what is said, though it does not concern you? Or, if you remain silent and in modest attention to your duty, what would be your interior life, if you let your thoughts wander from God? I once heard a silent person say that she was listening to everything around her, and making her Judas reflections on everything that was said and done; and another, that she delighted in silence because she could be thinking of her dear people.

And she ended wisely, "But you know better than that."[56]

In another conference Elizabeth kindly but relentlessly exposed the pretensions of self that sapped all good at its source. "You wish so much to be good and to please our dear Lord", she acknowledged with compassion, "that you will not be tired if I tell you what the spiritual guide says of the obstacles to our interior life." Note that she herself makes no pretensions to originality. Her teaching was accepted ascetism of the spiritual masters, which she had absorbed in spiritual direction and reading; but how vividly she salted it with her eye and ear for the homely and simple, the colorful, telling word or phrase! "The first", she continued, "is the little knowledge we have of ourselves and our faults; for, as by an interior life we wish to be united to Our Lord, a pure heart must be prepared, in which He may reign as in His own Kingdom. Self-love does not like to hear it, but our heart is very corrupt, and we must do continued violence to our bad nature to keep it in order."

Elizabeth would not leave her Sisters the false peace engendered by their agreement with so general a statement but uncovered one by one specific evils they were forced to recognize in themselves: "Our love of God is always opposed by our self-love", she stated flatly, our love of one another by the miserable pride and pretension which creates jealousy, rash judgment, and the pitiful dislikes and impatience which so often trouble us and wound charity. Curiosity, too, which keeps us engaged in what is doing and saying, brings home many a foolish companion for our thoughts, to break the silence and peace Our Lord desires to find in us. Who that reflect on their own nature can doubt of its corruption and misery? You know how unwilling we are to deny ourselves, how unwilling to be reproved or contradicted, how trifling a thing will make us sad, how we delight to be commended, while, with a sort of natural cruelty, we see blame and fault in others which we are scarcely willing to excuse.

Elizabeth then asked the totally honest question, drew the uncompromised conclusion:

How should we live an interior life until some of our natural rubbish is removed? How walk valiantly with Our Savior, dragging our foolish attachments after us, and ready to faint if the least weight of His cross presses on us? The less sensible we are of our misery the greater our evil is, for an immortified soul cannot bear to hear the truth nor to be reproved even for its evident faults; so it remains buried in its darkness, and the enemy tries to double its blindness, while, sick and weak, it scarcely struggles against its imperfections, much less thinks of entering the sanctuary of our interior life.[57]

Having exposed the maladies they would recognize, Elizabeth proceeded to the remedy: "You will never receive any lively impressions of grace until you overcome . . . dissipation of mind. If you are ever so fervent at your prayers, or desire ever so much to be good, it will be all like putting hartshorn in a bottle and leaving the cork out. What will it be worth?" The echo of the parables of her Lord was here. "So all the prayers, readings and good talk you love so much will be to little purpose, unless you place a sentinel at the door of your heart and mind. You often lose in ten minutes by your dissipation of mind more than you had gained a whole day by mortification."[58]

Elizabeth showed also how this lack of self-control at the source could ravage the entire spiritual structure built so laboriously. "How is it that many of us keep the rule as to the letter of it", she asked with a holy exasperation,

> and also look pious enough—there is no want of good will, nor idleness indulged—and in a house where it would seem so easy to become saints, you would say, what is the matter? Why are we not saints? Why is there so little progress in perfection, or rather, why are so many tepid, heavy, discouraged, and going along more like slaves in a workhouse than children in their own home and the house of their Father? Why? Because we do not watch over our interior, do not watch the impulse of nature and grace in our actions, nor avoid the occasions of the habitual faults we live in when it is in our power, or keep a good guard on ourselves when it is not. Frequent indulgence of useless thoughts, inconsiderate words, expressions of natural feelings and changes of temper, all stand at variance with our sweet interior life, and stop the operation of divine grace, too often indeed to grieving the divine Spirit and sending Him away.[59]

Elizabeth was particularly concerned that the novices and young Sisters should get started early on the right road: "Young people especially should fight cheerfully, since Our Lord has so kindly called you in the morning of your days, and not exposed you to the anguish and remorse we feel after so many years of sin", she pleaded. "It moves my very soul to see you young ones taken and sheltered by Our dear Lord, and yet you often look ungrateful . . . can you expect to go to heaven for nothing? Did not Our dear Savior track the whole way to it with His tears and Blood? —and yet you start at every little pain."[60]

Elizabeth well knew the sincerity of her listeners, however, and the weakness of human nature and did not fail to remind them of a traditional help and safeguard always at hand: "The rule given us for securing the heavenly practice of pure intention is to be careful of our morning offering, which seals the whole day; since Fénelon says, that after it is made fully and sincerely, if we should forget to renew it from hour to hour—as good souls commonly do—and do not retract it by any act of our will—if no mortal sin comes in the way—our first good offering secures all we do for the day. What a comfort that is!"[61]

The most agonizing form of mortification endured by Elizabeth Seton was one she shared with all the saints, indeed, with all good souls earnestly persevering in the struggle for perfection—aridity. It is sometimes a lassitude of soul, sometimes the searching for a hidden God, sometimes a blankness of spirit, sometimes a positive distaste for devotion, sometimes an aching depression, sometimes the shadow of quiet despair, but always an anguish of mind and soul. Elizabeth suffered it in its various disguises, often nurtured by physical weakness and the relentless illness that ate at her lungs or by the pangs and disappointments of natural and spiritual motherhood.

This scourge attacked Elizabeth's unremitting efforts to practice the highest virtue. "I am atom! You are God! Misery all my plea!" she cried piteously to her Lord.

> So few saved! If we are lost, are You less justified? The patience so long waiting, less adorable? And the soul, burying itself in the chaos of mystery, always rested in stupidity within; but without, played with children, amused with the Sisters, yielding to all minutiae, attentive to all necessities. . . . Not one spark of grace can the soul discern in it all, but rather a continuation of the original fault, of desire to do, to be loved, to please! And so far from the simplicity of grace which would turn every instant to gold, it felt ashamed when [it] returned to the tabernacle, as if it had played the fool, or acted like those women who try to please company and show their ill humors at home."[62]

Yet, with the sure instinct of the wholly dedicated soul, helped perhaps by the example of the great heroines of her spiritual reading—like St. Teresa of Avila, who endured more than twenty years of complete aridity yet never neglected a prayer, a devotion, or a duty though "not one spark of grace can the soul discern in it all"—St. Elizabeth clung faithfully to prayer and to work.

"Poor, poor poverino, obliged to preach", she lamented to her director, Bruté, at a time when illness weighed her down.

If you knew only one half my reluctance to give an instruction or a catechism (formerly the heart's delight), it seems to me even yourself would be tempted to turn away with disgust from the ungrateful culprit: but the Dearest says, "You shall, you must, only because I will it; trust your weak breast and turning head to Me; I will do all." And *Sam* is so cruel, whenever there is an evident success he pushes and says, "See how they are affected, how silent and attentive; what respect, what look of love!"—and tries to make distractions in every way. The poor, poor soul doesn't even look towards him, but keeps direct forward with Our Dearest, but with such a heavy, heavy heart at this vile mixture.

So, in the refectory sometimes, the tears start and the weakness of a baby comes over me, but Our Dearest again says, "Look up, if you had your little morsel alone, of another quality, no pains of body or reluctance to eat, what part would I have in your meal? But here is your place, to keep order, direct the reader, give example, and eat cheerfully the little you can take—in the spirit of love, as if before My tabernacle. I will do the rest. Abandon all." Abandon all! All is abandoned! But pray, pray for your poor one continually.[63]

Elizabeth, with her native good sense and spiritual sight, recognized her torments as temptations and dealt with them accordingly, but with what heroism and humility! "Yet it might be a grace," she admitted,

for as often He saw, it was no more in choice to hinder these evaporations than to stop the giddiness of my head in a fever. And they [the Sisters] are so loving, so fixed on Mother's every look, clouds or sunshine, so depending, sometimes I would shudder at the danger of such a situation if it was not clear as light that it is a part of the materials He takes for His work; and so little did He prepare the composition that He knows, if nature was listened to, I would take a blister, a scourging, any bodily pain, with a real delight, rather than speak to a human being—that heavy sloth which, hating exertion, would be willing to be an animal and die like a brute in unconsciousness! O, my Father, all in my power is to abandon and adore. How good He is to let me do that![64]

Elizabeth once expressed it in another way, extraordinary for its ecstasy amid the dejection and pain of divided human nature: "It is not the soul that is guilty of all this: The evil spirit is most active, it is true; but the good one sits in anguish at the foot of the cross, looking over all this desolation, adoring, subjecting, abandoning all to Him, seeing only Him, annihilating itself and all creatures before Him, saying *amen* to the resounding *alleluias,* and willing any moment to go into hell rather than add one more offense to the mountain it has already laid upon Him."[65]

Nowhere does Elizabeth ask that the persistent sadness of soul that she hid from the world be lifted from her. Early in her final years of illumination and union, she deliberately made her choice. "Understand, Blessed," she asked Father Bruté,

> and let not your too kind, too patient, heart *in its turn* "be sad." The sadness of mine I cherish as a grace, and do hope to have it to my *last hour,* because it makes me so watchful that I cannot open my lips since St. Raphael's Day without fear. A blessed fear! Would that I had had it these forty years—how short *my account* would be! And be assured that sorrowful mixture which works in every prayer, *sleeping* or waking, and asks our God continually, "Am I indeed in full charity with *all?* Pure, delicate, sincere charity?"—is no work of temptation; because, after the look over the whole and repeated act of contrition (such as poor I can offer) I give up all to Our dear God of mercy and compassion.

She strove to share her choice with her Sisters to alert them to the "grace", to instill in them the "blessed fear", she continued. "Besides, it is a community grace, for I have said to our Betsy and Margaret since: 'Do you know what you do? Mind—I have agonies of soul for less than that.' They both are quite too easy, as well as myself, on this edge of mortal sin. O my God, if He was not my God, I should go *crazy* in *head* as well as the poor body!"[66]

The sense of sin, as has been noted, pervaded Elizabeth's life of grace. It was not a scrupulousness or an exaggeration. It was the realism of the saints. Certainly St. Elizabeth Ann's consciousness of imperfection kept her in constant sorrow and penitence. "You see I say not a word to you of my poor interior world", she once broke off a recital of local and community news to Bruté.

> The poor little atom in darkness, clouds and continual miseries— going like a machine in the beautiful round of graces—a sad month, the past—but yet another begun in the same stupidity and weariness of soul and body. Communion itself but a moment of more indulgence for this state of torpor and abandonment, *wanting all* and *asking nothing* —for after so much asking and so much granted, to remain still the same unfaithful thing so long! Poor, poor soul, where will it end? *There* the point of *dreadful* uncertainty. I look over to the little Sacred Wood, then up to the clear vault—all is silent. Poor, poor soul![67]

The truly terrible cross and mortification of soul called aptly by spiritual writers the "dark night" is described by Elizabeth Seton in a paragraph that is chilling in its simple directness: "Waiting on a table opposite the door of the chapel, looking at the tabernacle"— this fixing of the sacred place of abandonment has its own cold terror—

> the soul appeals to Him if this is not a daily martyrdom. I love and live, and love and live, in a state of separation indescribable. My being and existence, it is true, are real, because I meditate, pray, conduct the community, etc., and all this with regularity, resignation and singleness of heart; but yet, this is not I, it is a sort of machinery, no doubt acceptable to the compassionate Father, but it is a different being from that in which the soul acts. In meditation, prayer, Communion, I find no soul; in the beings around me, dearly as I love them, I find no soul; in that tabernacle I know He is, but I see not, feel not; a thousand deaths might hang over me to compel me to deny His Presence there, and I would embrace them all rather than deny it an instant; yet it seems that He is not there for me—and yesterday, while for a few minutes I felt His Presence, it was only to make me know that Hell was gaping under me, and how awful His judgment would be."[68]

There is nothing to be said in the face of such utter penitential and mortified suffering; but, how joyful to remember that Elizabeth's last words were the prayer of the suffering Pius VI, whose depths of meaning she had savored and probed daily in her dying months: "May the most just, the most high and the most amiable Will of God be in all things fulfilled, praised and exalted above all forever."[69]

7

"A KIND OF JOHN THE BAPTIST"

St. Elizabeth Ann's brother-in-law once described her to her grandchildren as "a kind of John the Baptist".[1] His description was apt, for she was indeed a voice crying in the wilderness of a new land, "Make straight the way of the Lord." That she felt this mission and its starkness was evident in her joy at the arrival of the first Vincentians in America: she received holy Communion, she told Bruté, and "directed those of the Sisters to thanks for the blessed missioners sent to enlighten our savage land".[2] She was herself a born missioner; her life was wholly apostolic in its efforts and its fruits. It was her predestination.

It has been noted that saints are canonized not for what they do but for what they are. Yet what they do and what they are are profoundly interrelated: holiness of soul spilling over in good works, as creation is the superabundance of God's goodness, and the good works continuously influencing and building up holiness of soul. Both holiness and good works express themselves in apostolates that are at first the paths and then the fruits of vocations or callings.

St. Elizabeth Ann Seton had two essential vocations or callings, first to the married state and then to the religious life, and numerous apostolates flowed from each. When she was a married woman, her main apostolates were private, personal and intimate, not only to be a good wife and mother in the temporal sphere but also to be a bearer of salvation to her husband and children.

The love of Elizabeth and Will Seton was mutual and deep. Away on business, he could only wish "that tomorrow was come, that might bring me nearer to that little heart";[3] and she could assure him that his children "cannot understand that Papa is not to come, nor tomorrow, nor next day, nor the day after—that is for their mother to feel".[4] On her last visit to his grave in Livorno, she "wept plentifully over it", she told his sister Rebecca, "with the unrestrained affection which the last sufferings of his life, added to the remembrance of former years, had made almost more than human. When you read my daily memorandums since I left home, you will feel what my love has been and acknowledge that God alone could support it by His assistance through such proofs as have been required of it."[5] Years later she recalled: "It seemed that I loved him more than anyone could love on earth."[6]

For all the love between Elizabeth and Will Seton, it was unrequited in their lack of sharing fully and mutually in the love of God. A good and upright man, William Seton was a nominal Christian and no more. He was tolerant enough of his wife's devotion, but it was her constant complaint to Rebecca that "Willy does not understand".[7] His lack of understanding provoked her, on at least one occasion, to impatience and sarcasm. "Our H[enry] H[obart] was at *St. Mark's* instead of St. Paul's," she informed Rebecca, "and Willy says those who heard him said he was a great contrast to the gentleman *we had,* who had given them, in the morning, a *schism* sermon. Surely *H. H.* knew nothing of *schism* yesterday! Willy regretted very much he did not hear him. *Regrets are idle things.*"[8]

There was a change in Will's attitude, to which his rapidly declining health may have contributed, two months before the fatal voyage to Italy; that it was important is evident from Elizabeth's excitement. "Willy says he *will dine at home* tomorrow, with a significant smile", she told Rebecca. "I shall be too happy if he means to keep his promise *freely* and without any persuasion from me."[9] Hard on this came another note, detailing further developments that seem to be concerned, not so much with Will's going to church—there are indications that he did not neglect such an amenity—but with his approaching the Sacrament: "Since *a quarter* before three I have been, oh, how happy! Come, come, 'Soul's Sister,' *let us bless the day together—one body, one spirit, one hope, one God*—the Father of *all!* I think our Willy will go—he has not left me for five minutes since yesterday dinner, and has had *Nelson*[10] in his hands very often. If he does, what a dinner will *today's* be to me!"[11] And then, when the Reverend Hobart had come to visit and share her joy: "I told him the last twenty-four hours were the happiest I had ever seen or could ever expect, as the most earnest wish of my heart was fulfilled. Dear Rebecca, if you had known how sweet last evening was—Willy's heart seemed to be nearer to me for being nearer to His God. From absolute weariness of body I fell asleep at *eleven,* and left him with *Nelson* in his hand."[12]

It was not, however, the ultimate, for some twelve days into their shared anguish in the *lazaretto,* Elizabeth wrote of her dying husband in her *Journal:*

My William's soul is so humble, it will hardly embrace that faith, its only resource. At any time, whom have we but our Redeemer? But when the spirit is on the brink of departure, it must cling to Him with increased force, or where is it? Dear William, it is not from the impulse of terror you turn to your God. You tried and wished to serve Him long before this trial came. Why, then, will you not consider Him as the Father who knows all the different means and dispositions of His children, and will graciously receive those who come to Him by that way which He has appointed? You say your only hope is in Christ; what other hope do we need? He says that the first effects he ever felt from the calls of the Gospel, he experienced from our dear H[obart]'s pressing the question in one of his sermons: "What avails gaining the whole world and losing your own soul?" The reflections he made when he returned home were, "I toil and toil, and what is it? What I gain destroys me daily, soul and body. I live without God in the world, and shall die miserably." Mr. F. D., with whom he had not been in habits of business, offered to join him in an adventure; it succeeded far beyond their expectations. Mr. F. D. said, when they wound it up: "One thing, you know, I have been long in business—began with very little—have built a house and have enough to build another. I have generally succeeded in my undertakings and attribute all to this: That, whether they are great or small, I always ask a blessing of God, and look to that blessing for success." William says, "I was struck with shame and sorrow that I had been a heathen before God. *These* he called his two warnings, which awakened his soul, and speaks of them always with tears. Oh, the promises he makes, if it please God to spare him![13]

Elizabeth need not have worried over this "humble" soul, whom suffering and the inevitability of death had brought face to face with truth and who was only passing through the last phase of clinging without conviction to deceptive hopes and fruitless promises. Another two weeks, and the journey to peace was completed. On December 12, the doctor arrived, and William, "as soon as he saw him, told him he was not wanted, but I must send for him who would minister to his *soul*", Elizabeth recorded sadly, but, "My William looked in silent agony at me, and I at him, each fearing to weaken the other's strength. At the moment, he drew himself towards me and said, 'I breathe out my soul with you.' "[14]

From that moment on, Will's only concern was to prepare himself well to meet God: "No sufferings, nor weakness, nor distress (and from these he is never free in any degree) can prevent his following me daily in prayer, the Psalms and generally large readings of the Scriptures", Elizabeth wrote, herself in newfound peace. "If he is a little better, he enlarges his attention. If worse, he is more eager not to lose a moment. . . . [He] often talks of his darlings, but most, of meeting, one family, in heaven."[15]

Despite Elizabeth's heartsore human grief, how filled with joy was her soul to watch Will run now so swiftly in search of God. "Was so impatient to be gone that I could scarcely persuade him to wet his lips, but continued calling his Redeemer to pardon and release Him", she wrote of his truly blessed deathbed.

Every promise in the Scriptures and prayer I could remember I continually repeated to him, which seemed to be his only relief. When I stopped to give him anything: *"Why do you do it? What do I want? I want to be in heaven. Pray, pray for my soul....*" At four, the hard struggle ceased. Nature sank into a settled sob: "My dear wife—and little ones—My Christ Jesus, have mercy and receive me," was all I could distinguish; and again, repeated, "My Christ Jesus," until a quarter past seven, when the dear soul took its flight to the *Blessed Exchange* it so much longed for.[16]

While William Seton may be said to have had little to do with his children's spiritual upbringing in life, his truly holy death surely did much to make up for it, especially as a sacrifice and unceasing prayer before God both for their salvation and in support of their mother, who now had the awesome responsibility of both their upbringing and their salvation entirely and alone. It struck her most forcibly as she rode out of the cemetery in Livorno, "Poor, high heart . . . in the clouds, roving after my William's soul and repeating: 'My God, you are my God'; and so I am now alone in the world with You and my little ones"—yet to be alone with Him was everything, for "you are my Father, and doubly theirs".[17]

Some months later, as Elizabeth was struggling toward the truth of the Catholic Faith, she asked the Blessed Virgin "to obtain peace for my poor soul that I may be a good mother to my poor darlings".[18] To be a good mother had always been as paramount with her as to be a good wife; now that her children were orphans, it overrode all. They held priority in everything, temporal and spiritual. She made this very clear when the religious life was opening out before her and a spiritual motherhood was to be added to her and especially pondered it when the moment of truth arrived in the adoption of a permanent Rule. "The thought of living out of our valley would seem impossible if I belonged to myself," she told Julia Scott, "but the dear ones have their first claim, which must ever remain inviolate. Consequently, if at any time the duties I am engaged in should interfere with those I owe to them, I have solemnly engaged with our good Bishop Carroll, as well as my own conscience, to give the darlings their right, and to prefer their advantage in everything."[19] There was no ambiguity as to what their "right" and "advantage" entailed. "By the law of the Church I so much love," she assured Catherine Dupleix, "I could never take an obligation which interfered with my duties to them, except I had an independent provision and guardian for them, which the whole world could not supply to my judgment of a mother's duty."[20] And she asked Archbishop Carroll, in reference to the Daughters of Charity, who were expected from France to train the infant community in the Rule of St. Vincent, "How can they allow me the uncontrolled privileges of a mother to my five darlings?"[21]

Elizabeth had especially cultivated religion in her children from their births. There is abundant evidence of daily family prayers, even for the toddlers, and regular churchgoing as each grew old enough. Along with their schooling at home Elizabeth taught them the stories of David and Daniel and Judith and other biblical heroes and heroines. She led them in singing hymns. When she put them to bed, she laid her hand in blessing on them and made the sign of the cross on each little brow.[22]

When Anna was to make her first Communion, Elizabeth sent the little girl to stay with friends in town for a week of instruction and preparation at the hands of Augustinian Father Michael Hurley. "My darling daughter," she wrote lovingly to the child, "you must not be uneasy at not seeing me either yesterday or today. Tomorrow I hope to hold you to my heart, which prays for you incessantly that God may give you grace to use well the precious hours of this week.... Remember that Mr. Hurley is now in the place of God to you. Receive his instructions as from heaven, as no doubt the dear Savior has appointed them as the means of bringing you there."[23] That Anna kept to these and to her mother's instructions brought her through a teenage infatuation in absolute innocence, as Elizabeth learned unimpeachably and confided raptly to Julia Scott: "Music of heaven—that my darling should have had the virtue and purity of an angel in the first dawn of youthful and ardent affection (for she certainly is not without passion) is a joy to her Mother, which a Mother only can know."[24]

A typical birthday note to Catherine, who was as often called Josephine, her confirmation name, in the family circle, read:

> Birthday of my Josephine, and Mother's heart rejoices. It will look a little to the uncertainty of her crown, yet the good angel looks so smiling and points to the tabernacle. How can I help hoping my dear one will be safe? But, my darling, you must renew every good resolution, and keep close by your Good Shepherd. You know, the little lamb only stepped aside to crop the spear of grass, and then a little farther, and a little farther, 'till it could no longer hear the voice of the Shepherd; and then, when entangled in briars and thorns—you know the rest. My dear, dear one, think well of the little lamb. And take care of our dear little lamb, our little limping dear one. Oh, yes, take care and be a good angel to her! Bless, bless you forever![25]

To Rebecca, the "little limping dear one", Elizabeth wrote in the same affectionate vein before a Communion day: "My own child of eternity: With the little pen I answer my dear every day dearer little darling, how much I desire she should go and unite still closer with Our Only Beloved.... Make your careful preparation of the purest heart you can bring Him, that it may appear to Him like a bright little Star at the bottom of a fountain. O my Rebecca! Child of eternity, let peace and love stay with you in your pains, and they will lighten and sweeten them all."[26]

Elizabeth surely had no intention of foisting a religious life on any of her children, as she once protested humorously to Mrs. Scott about the girls, "Dearest Julia, you talk of making nuns like making bread. How can I make my dear ones love the life I love ...?"[27] It was solid piety she wished to pass on to them; what they were to do with it was up to God and themselves. It is true that Anna died in her mother's community, and Catherine became a Sister of Mercy long after her mother's death, but these were their, not their mother's, doings.

Indeed, Elizabeth confided to Julia, "I never look beyond year to year for either myself or them, as you know how much my constitution was long ago impaired, and my children have the most marked symptoms of our family complaint, and look forward themselves with cheerfulness and pleasure to an early reunion where there is no separation—especially the girls."[28] It was a hardheaded appraisal and revealed an exceptional frankness between mother and children.

When Rebecca's illness was in an advanced stage, Elizabeth sent her, in a last desperate measure, to a famous doctor in Philadelphia. Knowing how frightened the child would be at the separation, the mother tried to keep close to her by daily accounts of everything that went on at home. However, she did not hesitate to close one such letter with these exalted words: "My Rebecca, we will at last unite in His eternal praise, lost in Him, you and I, closer still than in the nine months so dear when, as I told you, I carried you in my bosom as He in our Virgin Mother's—then, no more separation."[29] The little country girl was, of course, enchanted by the great city where she visited "the museum, the Bank of Pennsylvania, Bank of the United States, the water works and I do not know where else"; but—her mother's true daughter—"What was better than all, Sister Rose took me to the poor house. You must know what a coward I am, as you have experienced me. I do not dare to think of my own sufferings after having seen theirs, though Sister Rose tells me I have seen but the best part of it."[30]

Elizabeth watched over Rebecca's soul as carefully as her wasted body to the last. "Poor beloved!" The mother wrote Father Bruté five months before the child's death. "We examine much together if she is in the good disposition of *the Will.* She is so *sure*—only she says, 'Perhaps I indulge my feelings too much, not staying in bed at night, but I do suffer so in it.' Strange indulgence! Yet do pray for the poor lamb: it has so many little old and even saucy ways of pride, pretension, etc. (Seton maladies)."[31]

Dearly as Elizabeth's sons, William and Richard, loved her, they were too restless of nature to want to remain in the valley she loved. They were eager to try the world, and their mother was too sensible to prevent them. But advise and guide and pray she did. "Be not, my dear one, so unhappy as to break wilfully any command of our God", she begged William on his first venture abroad, "or to omit your prayers on any account. Unite them always to the only merits of Our Jesus and the maternal prayers of Our Mother and His. With them you will always find your own poor, poor Mother's. You cannot even guess the incessant cry of my soul to them for you." She grew more agitated as she wrote:

Don't say Mother has the rest to comfort her. No, no, my William. From the first moment I received you in my arms and to my breast you have been consecrated to God by me, and I have never ceased to beg Him to take you from this world rather than you should offend Him or dishonor your dear soul; and, as you know, my stroke of death would be to know that you have quitted that path of virtue which alone can reunite us forever. Separation, everything else, I can bear—but that, never. Your Mother's heart must break, if that blow falls on it.[32]

Richard was most irresponsible and therefore more of a worry to his mother. "Richard . . . does not give poor Kit and me as much comfort in a year as one of your letters", she told William. "His heart is not turned like yours, my son, and I dread, yet hope, everything. . . . You may guess if I have any other hope but to look up to God, your Father and mine."[33] Four years later she was still hoping, still "looking up". "You can have no idea of our anxiety to hear from you", Elizabeth scolded in a letter to Richard, who was then with the Filicchis in Livorno. "Six, seven, eight months pass without one line. . . . What a beautiful consolation, my soul's Richard, it would be to me if you could write me in full sincerity before the Searcher of Hearts and not merely to comfort mine: 'Mother, I preserve my faith amidst all the dangers and scandals I meet—your Faith, Mother, the one so dear to you.' "[34]

Some weeks later, when Richard had finally written, it was only to cast down his mother's soul. He was "full of schemes about settling on the Black River", she confided to a friend, "black indeed will it be to him if he carries it through. He says, 'Commerce is a dead loss of time at present.' Poor fellow, I fear his faith is dead by the whole tenor of his letters; yet he puts change aside till another year. So, we will see. Nothing from William. You hear my sighs, and they go to your dear heart, I know; but never mind, my Ellen, Our God will pity."[35] And she besought Father John Hickey, "You pray, I hope for my poor, very poor, dear boys. My tears for them smart more and more day and night."[36] She was dying now, which made her heartbreak all the more poignant.

Elizabeth did her best to give the three children who would survive her a start in life. She sent Catherine to visit with friends and relatives in Philadelphia and New York that the girl might get to know the wide world outside the convent school in Emmitsburg. Elizabeth left Catherine at the end to the care of General Robert Goodloe Harper and his wife. Elizabeth prevailed on the faithful Filicchi brothers to train both her sons for business, though neither entered it. She importuned her many influential friends in behalf of William's commission in the United States Navy, much as she dreaded the possible effect on his soul.

There was Elizabeth's constant, chief concern—her children's souls. She felt, of course, the natural maternal pull on her heart, a pull aggravated by their orphanhood and their far from normal upbringing amid school children and nuns. But the importance of their salvation was supreme, and she never left off urging it at every possible opportunity, on every possible occasion. She put it all in proper perspective in a few lines to Antonio Filicchi concerning William: "I cannot hide from Our God, though from everyone else I must conceal, the perpetual tears and affections of boundless gratitude which overflow my heart when I think of him secure in his *Faith* and your protection. Why I love him so much I cannot account, but own to you, my Antonio, all my weakness. Pity and pray for a mother attached to her children through such peculiar motives as I am to mine. I purify it as much as I can, and Our God knows it is their souls alone I look at."[37]

The mother's prayers and tears were neither requited nor rewarded while she lived, but they were not wasted. Richard died at sea, just two years after his mother; it was a noble death of a fever contracted by nursing a Protestant clergyman back to health. William lived into old age and died with his children around him, among them a priest (and future archbishop) and a nun.

There are curious hints or "prophecies" of Elizabeth Seton's ultimate religious vocation even in her early life. She writes of "passionate wishes that there were such places in America as I read of in novels, where people could be shut from the world and pray, and be good always. Many thoughts of running away to such a place over the seas, in disguise, working for a living."[38] Young romanticism beyond a doubt, yet suggestive of an inchoate yearning that took form and intensity bit by bit in later years and the proper environment.

More significant, however, was Elizabeth's sacred bond with her sister-in-law Rebecca Seton, a rarely spiritual soul. The two became quickly "soul's sisters", and their mutual devotions and good works earned for them the indulgent nickname of "Protestant Sisters of Charity". When the two came together under the direction of the earnest curate of Trinity Church, they leaped forward in a holy bond that was a nascent form of religious community, a "sacred circle" to which they later invited Catherine Dupleix. As the older, and even then more advanced or secure, Elizabeth was the "superior" who did not hesitate to admonish when the occasion called for it. When Rebecca had broken their pact to remain at home in prayerful reflection on Sacrament Sunday by reluctantly fulfilling a social obligation, Elizabeth scolded her gently but firmly in words that, for all their apparent rigor, made a certain religious sense: "The misfortune of the afternoon will, I hope, be a lesson for life to my darling sister", she wrote soothingly,

> that you should never violate the strict rule, not to leave home on any persuasion on Sacrament Sunday, and to say openly to whoever may request it that it is your rule. It can never be a breach of civility or seem unkind . . . if you say it with a firmness of one who has been at His table who refreshes and strengthens the soul in well-doing. I have often asked myself the question: Why should anyone be more earnest and prevailing with me for a trifle or a thing of no consequence in itself, than I am in maintaining the thing I know to be right and that touches the interest of my soul's peace.[39]

It was to Rebecca that Elizabeth poured out her heart from the abyss of her sufferings in the *lazaretto* of Livorno, to Rebecca that she confided her wonder and delight in the dawning faith she found among her newfound Catholic friends in the months that followed, to the dying Rebecca that she went in dismay directly on landing home in New York. Elizabeth's special messages had fallen on willing eyes and ears, and although the dying girl could not do anything to formalize them—Elizabeth herself was not ready for such a step— she showed her heart by gasping faithfully the words of Ruth to Naomi, "Your people are my people, your God, my God."[40]

A further indication of Elizabeth's early influence as a leader in religion and things of the soul was the immediate impact her conversion to Catholicism had on her youngest sisters-in-law, Cecilia and Harriet Seton, both teenagers, and their cousin Eliza Farquhar.[41] The rest of the family reacted with angry and intense hostility, and the Farquhar girl soon lost all will to resist them, and even Harriet faltered for a time. Cecilia was not to be intimidated, young as she was—fifteen—and Elizabeth became her spiritual guide, bringing down on herself the Setons' fury and, indeed, the opprobrium of the whole town. Despite really harrowing persecution Cecilia, with Elizabeth's encouragement and firm backing and the counsel of Father Cheverus, persevered, and on June 17, 1806, voluntarily left her family. "My dear Charlotte," she announced quietly to her sister in a note,

> in consequence of a firm resolution to adhere to the Catholic Faith, I left your house this morning; and can only repeat that, if in the exercise of *that* faith my family will again receive me, my wish is to return and give them every proof of my affection by redoubled care to please them and submission to their wishes in every point consistent with my duty to *Him* who claims my first obedience. Under these circumstances, whatever is the Providence of Almighty God for me, I must receive it with entire resignation and confidence in His protection—but in every case must be your affectionate sister, Cecilia.[42]

Three days later Cecilia was received into the Catholic Church. On April 29, 1810, she died at the age of twenty, the first of Mother Seton's religious daughters to be given back to God.

Harriet accompanied Cecilia to Baltimore when the latter went to join the Sisterhood, intending to return to New York to marry Elizabeth's half-brother Barclay Bayley, who was in Jamaica in the West Indies. When he proved faithless, the unhappy Harriet lingered on in Emmitsburg, where, under the understanding direction of Father Pierre Babade, she became a Catholic in September 1809. She had made her decision during a late-night visit to St. Mary's Church on the mountain of the same name two months before. Elizabeth has left a description of her "stealing up to the church by the light of a full moon, in deepest silence, her arms crossed upon her breast, and the moon's reflection full on her pale but celestial countenance. I saw the falling tears of love and adoration, while we said, first *Miserere* and then *Te Deum* which from her childhood had been our family prayers. Descending the mountain, she burst forth the full heart: 'It is done, my sister, I am a Catholic. The cross of Our Dearest is the desire of my soul. I will never rest till He is mine.' "[43] Although seemingly in the bloom of health, the girl was unexpectedly stricken with a kind of brain fever, lingered four weeks and died on December 22, 1809.

Elizabeth's role in these conversions was most appropriate, for her own long and hard conversion was the first giant step towards her religious vocation and public calling. The second was the series of trials it precipitated, trials that were in fact cleansing agents sweeping the past out of the way of her progress into the future: the ostracism of family and friends and ultimately the hostility of the whole city, which defeated her efforts to support her children and finally convinced her that she must leave New York for love of her children's very souls.

That God's intent was much more pervasive than one little family, however good and precious, is evidenced in the prophetic note that now appeared in the advices of Elizabeth's spiritual guides. "Your perseverance and the help of grace will finish in you the work which God has commenced", Father Matignon assured her, "and will render you, I trust, the means of effecting the conversion of many others."[44] And, since Elizabeth had evinced serious thought of fleeing to Montreal, he sought to dissuade her: "You are destined, I think, for some great good in the United States," he stated flatly, "and here you should remain in preference to any other location."[45]

These solemn words must have sounded fatefully in Elizabeth's ears, but she did not yet give them, or rather herself, undue importance, for she continued to press Antonio Filicchi with her thoughts of a religious future much more private in execution and effect. She seems to have alerted him to the possibility nearly a year before, when she wrote that she had "a little secret to communicate to you when we meet (a sweet dream of imagination)".[46] Now, she grew more specific in an allusion that has never been explained: "If you were now here, my dear brother, I think you would exert your friendship for us and obtain the so long desired refuge of a place in the order of St. Francis for your converts."[47]

From this time on Elizabeth's future outside of New York was roundly discussed and reasoned. The real call came from God in April 1808, when Father William Dubourg of Baltimore—as she told Julia Scott—"offered to give me a formal grant of a lot of ground ... and procure me immediately the charge of a half-dozen girls, and as many more as I can manage".[48] Elizabeth answered the call at once. The needed advice had been sought and opinions given long before, and only the opportunity had been awaited. She arrived in Baltimore to begin her life's work on the feast of Corpus Christi, June 16, 1808.

There was the momentary, and again curious, distraction of her meeting Samuel Cooper, who had come to Maryland to study for the priesthood, and their mutual attraction. However, Elizabeth had answered her call, and there was no turning aside. "You may be sure I have always considered him as a consecrated being—as he did me", she told Julia Scott, "and the only result of this partiality has been the encouragement of each other to persevere in the path which each had chosen."[49]

Elizabeth paid serious attention now to further prophecies and their importance for others. "It is expected I shall be the mother of many daughters", she wrote quite simply to Cecilia Seton. "A letter received from Philadelphia where my blessed father, our patriarch [Father Pierre Babade], now is on a visit, tells me he has found two of the sweetest young women, who were going to Spain to seek a refuge from the world—though they are both Americans, *Cecilia* and *May*—and now wait until my house is opened for them: next spring, we hope. He applies to me the Psalm in our Vespers: *The barren woman shall be the joyful mother of children,* and tells me to repeat it continually, which you must do with me, my darling."[50] The ultimate prophecy came, however, from the saintly Father, later Bishop, Cheverus of Boston. "I see already numerous choirs of virgins following you to the altar", he told her solemnly. "I see your holy order diffusing itself in the different parts of the United States, spreading everywhere the good odor of Jesus Christ and teaching by their angelical lives and pious instructions how to serve God in purity and holiness. I have no doubt, my beloved and venerable sister," he finished, echoing his friend Matignon, "that He who has begun this good work will bring it to perfection."[51]

Elizabeth herself was wonderfully happy in all that had come to pass, culminating in her first vows on the feast of the Annunciation and causing her to cry out to Julia Scott, "To speak the joy of my soul at the prospect of being able to assist the poor, visit the sick, comfort the sorrowful, clothe little innocents and teach them to love God".[52] These few words sum up the whole religious vocation of Elizabeth Ann Seton and reveal her as the spiritual daughter of St. Vincent de Paul she was to become in such perfection, and after her her own religious daughters. It had two main thrusts: The poor and education, and both were to be realized, although not at the same time.

From earliest childhood Elizabeth Seton had a heart for the poor, the sick, the helpless and unfortunate—a heart of total service, an apostle's heart. By her own testimony, at eight she took "delight in being with old people",[53] at twelve she loved to "nurse the children and sing little hymns over the cradle",[54] at eighteen, she recalled with amusement, she had "fine plans of a little country home, to gather all the little children round and teach them their prayers, and keep them clean, and teach them to be good".[55]

Grown up and married, Elizabeth helped found the Widows' Society in New York, an association of Protestant matrons who, in unwitting emulation of St. Vincent de Paul's Ladies of Charity, not only gave their own money and coaxed others to give, even begging from door to door, but also visited the poor in their homes, taking them food and clothing prepared and sewn with their own hands.[56]

Elizabeth was the first one called to the bedside of the sick and dying.[57] She was prompt to respond and brought the poor sufferers the consolations of religion along with the medicines and comfits. When the end had come and she could do no more, she stayed behind to console the bereft. She gave Eliza Sadler a graphic description of her ministrations to Julia Scott at the death of Julia's young husband: "I have not left her night or day during the excess of her sorrows, and such scenes of terror I have gone through as you nor no one can imagine. 'Tis past. Little Julia goes to Philadelphia next week where she is to fix her residence, as her family connections are all there. And I am once more home, ten thousand more times delighted with it than before, from witnessing the horrors of the separation and derangement in that of my friend."[58] Mrs. Sadler was herself to be the beneficiary of Elizabeth's solace three years later, when her own husband died. Now it was Julia's turn to learn from Elizabeth, "I have borne *my part* in the melancholy scene", and she was, "as seems my lot to be, her only earthly support."[59]

Charity did begin at home for Elizabeth, as the adage has it, often shouldering responsibilities thrust upon her that few others are called to assume. When her father-in-law died, leaving six children under eighteen, Elizabeth's husband, as the oldest, had to assume responsibility for them, and the young couple was forced out of the privacy of their first little home to care for the children in the more spacious Seton mansion. Even the generous-souled Elizabeth, who was but twenty-three at the time, admitted candidly that "for me, who so dearly loves quiet and a small family, to become at once the mother of six children [besides her own two and a third on the way] . . . is a very great change".[60] When the yellow fever struck New York that autumn, they all had to take refuge in the Seton country cottage, along with Will's sister Eliza Maitland and her brood, causing the young wife to remark ruefully to Julia Scott: "You may imagine that eighteen in [the] family, in a house containing only five small rooms, is rather more than enough."[61] She was not complaining, just stating facts, as she always did. Indeed, the Maitlands were often the objects of the Setons' charity; even when the Setons were themselves on the edge of poverty, they fed the unhappy family, "six in number . . . from our own storeroom and every day marketing, as no other part of the family will keep them from starving, or even in firewood".[62]

Elizabeth Seton learned from the poor, as God intended. She learned, first of all, a profound gratitude. "Had a two hours' visit from my widow Veley", she wrote in her *Journal,* "no work, no wood, child sick, etc.—and should I complain, with a bright fire within, bright, bright *moon* over my shoulder, and the darlings all well . . . ?"[63] It was a holy gratitude, for she remembered in later years that her Widows' Society made her "delight in the continual contrast of all my blessings with the miseries I saw, yet always resigning them".[64]

Elizabeth learned, as well, how to be poor in spirit and detached from her possessions. Preparing for the voyage to Italy for her husband's health, she took "delight in packing up all our valuables to be sold, enjoying the *adieu* to each article to be mine no more".[65]

Elizabeth learned that love of the poor had to come from a heart in love with God. As she was to tell her Sisters, "*We sanctify ourselves for others.*"[66] And she probed the sacred truth more deeply during the memorable retreat in preparation for the community's first vows: "The Daughters of Charity," she noted, "led by their Beloved into solitude, look at Him and their own souls with their most religious and loving thoughts, and express also to Him their concern for other souls.... Thy Kingdom come ... let Thy Kingdom be founded forever in our hearts—oh! we pledge them all to spread it also the most we can to others."[67] And the means right at hand, she assured the Sisters, was their own good example: "We must be a shining and brightning light of edification to all, that they may say, 'See how pure, holy and glorious is religion in the souls truly sanctified by its best spirit.' O my God, this is our vocation."[68]

This led naturally to the further lesson that love of the poor and their material relief must be entirely motivated by the holy desire for their eternal salvation. "And the souls of others, will we forget them?" the saint asked. "O my God! We are the Daughters of Charity. From our happy solitude we look to the misery of the souls at large, we know how many do not know Thee, do not serve Thee." Elizabeth had clear-sighted vision of both the physical and spiritual poverty of so many men and women (a spiritual poverty overwhelming in what is so often and so justly called the post-Christian age), and she was just as clear-sighted in recognizing her own and her Sisters' responsibility towards them: "Our name", she insisted, "devotes us to their service in any manner that we could truly serve them." But "we must bring them to the knowledge of and the practice of Thy holy religion, to the habits of a good life".

This, Elizabeth told her Sisters, was their goal, to be achieved through the relief of temporal ills: "We must display for them the tender compassion of Thy goodness, be the ministers of Thy providence for the relief of their miseries, a relief which disposes so well every heart to Thy better service."[69] After Elizabeth's death, her director Father Bruté marked this goal as central to the very existence of the community. "Round her assembled other hearts [as] worthy for zeal", he wrote. "With her they lived that life which shows to the world that light of holiness which Jesus Christ tells us we should offer to our brethen."[70] The most uncompromising lesson Mother Seton learned was that, no matter how her heart went out to the poor, no matter their priority in that same loving heart, no matter how eager she was to serve them, it was up to God whether she did so or not. The supreme example, a classic case of God's bending personal desires to the accomplishment of His Will, was the establishment of Elizabeth's life work itself.

There can be no doubt of what Elizabeth wanted. Father Dubourg, whom God had sent to guide her to the religious life and her ultimate apostolate, has testified that he "had thought for a long time of establishing the Daughters of Charity in America; and as the duties of this institute would be compatible with the cares of her family, [Mrs. Seton] expressed a most ardent desire of seeing it commenced and of being herself admitted into it."[71] When the Rule of the Daughters had arrived from Paris, and Elizabeth had read it carefully, she had "not a thought discordant"[72] with it. The poor are the portion of the Daughters of Charity, founded by that Father of the Poor, St. Vincent de Paul. But it was not to be her portion, or that of her community, at least in the beginning. The sole Vincentian work allowed them was to teach "little innocents ... to love God".[73] It is true that some poor children were educated free of charge in her school[74] and that the Sisters "had the entire charge of the religious instruction of all the country round" and were able to visit the sick, although Elizabeth admitted wistfully, "The villages round us are not very extensive."[75]

These ministrations were, nonetheless, "extras". The principal apostolate of Elizabeth and her Sisters was forced by circumstances away from the poor and towards the children of the well-to-do. She told her friend and benefactor the stark truth at New Year's in 1812: "The promising and amiable perspectives of establishing a house of plain and useful education, retired from the extravagance of the world," she wrote, "connected also with the view of providing nurses for the sick and poor, an abode of innocence and refuge of affliction, is, I fear, now disappearing under the pressure of debts contracted at its very foundation."[76]

God rewarded Elizabeth's loving docility, even in her lifetime. She was able to take over orphanages in Philadelphia in 1814 and in New York in 1817 and a free school in Philadelphia in 1818— all this despite Archbishop Carroll's considered prediction that

the Sisters would not be able to turn to such works for at least
a hundred years.[77] Elizabeth herself admitted, "Our orphan
asylums . . . promise more than we could have hoped."[78] Within a
few years of her death, the Sisters opened their first hospital; then
in quick succession came one new social work after another—
to the point that, just as the Church has named her father,
St. Vincent, "Patron of All Organizations of Charity", and her
mother, St. Louise de Marillac, "Patroness of All Christian Social
Workers", Elizabeth herself can well and truthfully be called the
Mother of Christian Social Work in America.

Although deprived of working personally and directly with
the poor, St. Elizabeth Ann continued to dote upon them in
thought and desire. On one occasion she reminded a former pupil
that Advent was "so sweet a season for comforting the poor and in
everyone, Our *coming Lord*".[79] On another occasion, she was
happy to send the news to Bruté, "So many of your mountain
children and poor, good Blacks came today for first Communion
instructions. They were told from the *pulpit*, all to repair to the
Sisterhood—so they came as for a novelty but we will try our
best . . . poor, dear souls so unconscious—!!!"[80] Sister Cecilia
O'Conway recalled some Sisters brightening Elizabeth's last days
with tales of their visits to "several poor round the mountains".
Elizabeth was so absorbed that, "finding one had yet something
more to tell, she eagerly said, 'O! do tell me, it delights me so
much to hear such things!' " And Sister Cecilia finished fondly,
"Yes, blessed soul, truly dear were the poor and unfortunate to
your heart."[81] It is fitting that the Church recognized at Elizabeth's
canonization her love for the poor and the apostolate to the poor
she planted in the hearts of her Sisters. "We pray", said Paul VI,
"that the Church in the United States will indeed be faithful to
her [Elizabeth's] mission on behalf of those who endure suffering
in various forms—spiritual and material poverty, sickness, loneliness,
lack of understanding, deprivation of rights—on behalf of those
in the margin of society, those without hope."[82]

The second, and in the beginning the dominant, thrust of
Mother Seton's religious vocation, Catholic education, also had

prophetic roots in her earlier Protestant life. By her own recollection, as a little girl she was forever teaching other children, especially about God.[83] Towards the end of 1798, she began her first "home school" for the youngest Seton girls, Harriet and Cecilia, because sending them out "through snow and wet will give me more trouble than keeping them at home".[84] As her own children grew, so did the family student body; after her return from Italy, they became her entire class.

That little parlor on Stone Street in lower New York was in a rudimentary sense the forerunner of every Catholic parish classroom in the United States. It was real education, not playacting. School began at ten o'clock each morning, and the subjects studied were "grammar, reading, writing, spelling of large and small words, marking, sewing and figures".[85] Even the prekindergarten tots recited "their lessons: little pieces, names of the United States, divisions of the globe, some of the commandments".[86] No teaching of Elizabeth Seton could be devoid of religion. Cecilia was especially apt in imitating Elizabeth's piety, and there is preserved a little packet of religious sayings and admonitions: "To Cecilia B. Seton from her own sister, E.A.S., 19th November, 1802."[87] Following her conversion, Elizabeth involved herself with schools begun by a Mr. White and a Mr. Harris, both Protestants, but the bigotry of the town towards her helped defeat the enterprises.

Elizabeth was surely ready when the call to Catholic Baltimore came "at this very moment of solicitude for our destination when the present means fails", and she rightly attributed it to "the Providence that overrules us".[88] What gave her most joy was that the house provided for her was "almost joining the chapel . . . Mass from daylight to eight . . . Vespers and Benediction every evening",[89] and that her school was to be a Catholic school. She heartily concurred with her patron, Father Dubourg, that "there are in the country, and perhaps too many, mixed schools, in which ornamental accomplishments are the only objects of education; we have none that I know where their acquisition is connected with, and made subservient to, *pious* instruction — and such a one you certainly wish yours to be."[90]

Elizabeth herself put it even more directly when she reminded Antonio Filicchi that "the subject of my last [letter] to you . . . so nearly concerns all my hopes and expectations for this world, which is to do something—if ever so little—towards promoting our dear and holy faith".[91] In a letter to his brother Filippo, she specified her "plan of establishing an institution for the advancement of Catholic female children in habits of religion, and giving them an education suited to that purpose".[92]

From the beginning Elizabeth and her Sisters were happy in the apostolate God had substituted for their original plans. One of the Sisters has left a memorable record of that happiness in describing the first high Mass in the yet unfinished "White House" on March 19, 1810: "So poor was the little altar, that its chief ornaments were a framed portrait of Our dear Redeemer which Mother had brought with her from New York, her own little silver candlesticks, some wild laurel, paper flowers, etc.—yet what a happy, happy company, far from the busy, bustling scenes of a miserable, faithless world!"[93]

Hindsight makes plain God's purpose in directing Elizabeth Seton to the apostolate of Catholic education. It was essential for inculcating the Faith in a vast primitive land that would continuously expand its borders and welcome ever new hordes of immigrants. It was essential for protecting the faith of so many of these same immigrants and their children, cast ashore amid a populace in large measure hostile to the Catholic religion. In time the Catholic school became the bulwark and glory of the Church in America, developing into a unique and successful system of thorough secular and religious training. Mother Seton did not plan the system, but she provided the working model: the three children from St. Joseph's Parish, Emmitsburg, who were admitted to her day school on February 22, 1810, where they were taught by religious women and gratis formed the first of the parochial schools which were to spread in a defined network across America. It was something she did quite consciously, for Father Dubourg had assured her earlier that "far from objecting to your plan of opening a day school at St. Joseph's, Mr. David and myself beg it should be done without loss of time".[94]

Elizabeth was quick to see the hand of God, to recognize that this unforeseen emphasis on the apostolate of education enjoyed that "blessing and success which is the work of God alone".[95] Indeed, she foretold with great content its eternal worth in the "precious souls which we cherish and prepare in silence and under a rather common look of no pretension to go over our cities like a good leaven".[96] Pope Paul VI spoke the definitive and official word in telling the American bishops present in Rome for Elizabeth Seton's canonization how his thoughts "turn spontaneously to parochial and other Catholic schools in your nation. We bless the providence of God that raised up Mother Seton to inaugurate this important work. We render homage to those who have expended their lives to communicate Christ through the apostolate of the school, and to give to generations of young Americans true education imbued with Christian principles."[97]

On this same occasion the Holy Father had first of all paid tribute to the holy mother's all-embracing charism, her call to the religious life. It was as foundress of the first native Sisterhood in America that she provided the means of serving both the nation's poor and its school children. "The very meaning . . . of the canonization of St. Elizabeth Seton", the Pope said with notable emphasis,

> impels us to express our good wishes, filled with loving hope, for religious life in the United States. Through you, the bishops, we say to all the religious: "Let us keep our eyes fixed on Jesus, who inspires and perfects our faith" (Heb 12:2). Jesus, and Jesus alone, is our wisdom, our justice, our sanctification, our redemption (cf. I Cor 1:30).
>
> Through the powerful example of joyful love and of selfless service rendered by religious, may the young people of America again find attraction in Christ's invitation to follow Him and to be witnesses of the transcendence of His love. Our earnest prayer, therefore, for all religious is that they may base all their activity on the power of God and not on the deceptive wisdom of the world, and that they may recognize for their lives the absolute necessity of prayer and of the transforming power of

the Eucharist, source of all the Church's power (cf. *Sacrosanctum Concilium*, 10). After the shining example of Elizabeth Seton may they have renewed conviction that Christ offers them complete fulfillment in their vocation of consecrated love and ecclesial service.[98]

It would have been very difficult for Elizabeth Ann Seton, in her lifetime, to have imagined the Holy Father in faraway Rome even knowing her name, let alone extolling her as a model for religious.

Elizabeth took her academic duties as principal or headmistress very seriously, visiting each classroom every day and making a detailed study of each at least once a month, with particular attention to the quality of the teaching and the aptitude of the pupils.[99] As for her spiritual duty to instruct young souls, her wholehearted devotion to it was one of the chief contributions to her sainthood, for she was a constant, shining light to all, her sanctity not only illuminating what she taught but also showing concretely how to love God. The love that united Mother and little pupil-daughter is evident in the constant notes that passed between them, such as this: "Mother begs Our Lord to bless her dear Eliza that she may be an everblooming rose in His paradise. Come under the shawl this morning, and love and bless Our Jesus — your poor, unfortunate Mother."[100]

The instructions Elizabeth gave twice a week to the older girls made plain their purpose from the outset: "Your little Mother, my darlings, does not come to teach you how to be good nuns or Sisters of Charity, but rather I would wish to fit you for that world in which you are destined to live; to teach you how to be good . . . mothers of families."[101] Like her divine Master, she used parables, metaphors and similes to impress minds so young. Warning of the allurements of the world they were preparing for, she recounted how "the fable says that a butterfly asked an owl what she should do to keep from burning her wings, since she could never come to the candle without singeing them. The owl counselled her to abstain from looking even at the smoke of it. You will first burn your wings, poor little moth[s]", she drew the lesson, "before you will withdraw from the flame. In all these cases, there is more safety in our fear than in our strength; it is ever easier to abstain from such pleasures than to use them well."[102] The heart duly prepared for the reception of holy Communion she depicted as "a crystal vial filled with clear water, in which the least mote of uncleanness may be seen".[103] Her spiritual nurture of young souls was summed up in an unforgettable word of advice: "Love God, my dear children, and you may forget there is a hell."[104]

The bond of love forged was a lasting one, as evidenced by the extensive correspondence engendered by pupils long graduated seeking their Mother's advice in each new upsetting experience. To Sarah Caufmann of Philadelphia, troubled by a letter left by an admirer at her door, the Mother replied by asking,

> Is it not more simple and consistent to hear and answer its contents with the respect and gratitude due to an amiable being who gives us an unmerited preference, than to play the part of a proud woman receiving a homage she thinks her due? If you must *reject,* my precious child, do it with reason, and a candid statement of your reasons. Then, if they are approved or condemned, you will have acted like a Christian and your mind will be at peace, however painful the exertion—and reject you will, unless there is a fund of uncommon virtue in the person in question. Your poor little Mother can only pray for you, my beloved.[105]

Ellen Wiseman was especially beloved, and the two were faithful correspondents. "Try to keep all your intentions to Our Lord", Elizabeth advised this dear daughter. "When you go to your dearest companions, go in His name and send up the little sign to beg Him to stay with you, even *most* in your liveliest moments. Dearest Ellen, it will soon become so easy and so sweet, and when Death comes, O then the blessed practice will be your great consolation."[106] Once Elizabeth wrote Ellen in alarm, occasioned by a note which had warned her, "Pray for your Philadelphia children, Mother; they want it. *Kitty* Wiseman and R. Mallon alone resist the tide—Much as to say my Ellen goes with it. Oh, my God! What a hard world to steer through with innocence! My Ellen, chosen, beloved child of my heart, I must leave you to Our God. You are as far out of my reach as my soul's William is. What is all I can say? How can I even guess your trials, circumstances, affairs of the heart, temptations of all kinds? But my God will protect and save my beloved ones, I trust."[107] This trust, invoked over and over for those she loved, was well placed precisely because she placed it without faltering.

Two years later Elizabeth was rallying Ellen about confession: "Think how I would beg you, supplicate you, this day"—it was the feast of St. Peter, the holder of the keys—

> to keep you near to Him by the *only means,* and not let the wall of partition be raised again in your dearest heart as it was before our last happy meeting. Wake up your faith. You know Our Lord never meant us to mind who we go to, if they do but take us to Him. And the longer you stay back you well know the harder it is for you to go forward. And, alas, what does it end in? Dearest, to go through double trouble, pain and examens, which will not be pains of grace and merit, but of your own weakness and want of courage in delaying. Oh, do, dearest, write me you have been.[108]

The trust of her "old girls" gave Elizabeth great joy and encouraged her to urge them to even greater goodness because, as she said, "It is *you* young ones He delights in who have so many sacrifices to offer Him."[109] In return, she could reassure them with complete honesty that "Our Lord who sees the deep heart knows with what pleasure I would give my life to prove my true love to any of you".[110]

Mother Seton's love extended to the boys at Mount St. Mary's, personally and through her Sisters, whom she sent to do their laundry, mend their clothes and nurse them when they were sick. She was partial to the poor, whether in goods or in heart. She scraped together fifty dollars a year from her own meager funds to help pay the tuition of Charles Grim, son of a poor New York widow who had been her friend in former years. She tried to lighten the loneliness of little Jerome Bonaparte, left behind when his parents went to Paris at the command of his uncle Napoleon. "My dear Mother," the boy once wrote her earnestly, "I am very anxious to get an Agnus Dei before I go home, in order to preserve me in the vacations from the dangers that will surround me. . . . I will keep it as a memorial of kindness and love for your little child, who always thinks of you with respect and love", he continued with a child's instinctive trust in and attraction to goodness, "and who will think of you with gratitude also", he finished with a child's native slyness, "especially if I shall have an Agnus Dei from you as a present."[111] Elizabeth responded graciously: "Dear Jerome: It is a great pleasure to me to send you the Agnus Dei. I wish I had one handsomely covered; but you will mind only the virtues of the prayers Our Holy Father has said over it. I earnestly beg Our Lord to preserve you in the graces He has so tenderly bestowed on you", she continued, seizing on the boy's reason for the request to remind him, "take care yourself not to lose them. Pray for me, and I will for you. Your true friend, E.A.S."[112]

Elizabeth personally prepared many of the Mount boys for their first holy Communion. Her *Notebook* for February 2, 1813, records a meditation for the first Communion day of Michael de Burgo Egan, perhaps a summary of things she had taught him and his classmates as they made ready for this day: "Piety must be habitual, not by *fits*. It must be persevering, because temptations continue all our lives—and *perseverance* alone obtains the crown. Its means are—the presence of God—good reading, prayer, the Sacraments, good resolutions often renewed—the remembrance of our last ends—and its advantages—habits which secure our predestination, making our life equal, peaceable and consoling— leading to the heavenly crown where our perseverance will be eternal!!!"[113] The urging to perseverance and the means of assuring it are standard spiritual advice, but the stamp of deep perception growing out of holiness is on the sure theological insight that these habits *secure* predestination, and the recognition of its signs, an "equal, peaceable and consoling" life—imparted with the enthusiasm of holiness, the saint's habitual underlining and exclamation points.

Elizabeth's holiness was not lost on Egan and his companions. "I remember Dearest Mother's repeated expression of Faith and *Love*", he wrote Catherine Seton, long afterward.

> How well she possessed them. Faith enlightened her, Love inflamed her, and the more I reflect on it the more I perceive how justly she insisted on those two great virtues.... I cannot help thinking it is harder for a priest to get to heaven than anyone else — though indeed surrounded and loaded with graces — yet beset with dangers and overwhelmed with difficulties also.... Would to Our Lord I had some small share of that holy love which inflamed the heart of our Dear Mother—Love would sweeten everything—Love would triumph over everything.[114]

Egan's easy assumption that Elizabeth was *his* mother as well as her own Catherine's is in itself a lesson in the power of love.

Elizabeth's special affection was reserved for seminarians like Egan, and it grew out of her "religious respect for the ministers of the Lord",[115] cited by Bruté in a tribute after her death. She herself laid the ground for this "religious respect" in a letter to a young man who had left the Mount in a flurry of doubts as to his vocation. "My dear Smith, my heart has gone home with you", she assured him, "as a parent follows the child she loves when she sees it treading in uncertain steps, doubtful whether it will find the right way." She had no doubts herself:

> To be engaged in the service of our adored Creator, to be set apart to that service, and thereby separated from all the contentions, the doubts and temptations that surround the man whose lot is cast in the busy scene of the world, is in itself a sufficient plea on the side which I wish you to engage, but to be placed as a representative of God Himself, to plead for Him, to be allowed the exalted privilege of serving Him continually, to be His instrument in calling home the wandering soul and sustaining, comforting and blessing your fellow creatures, are considerations which bear no comparison with any other; and should lead you to consider the very possibility of your realizing

the hope they present as the most precious and valued gift this life can afford.

Much as Elizabeth wanted this young man to continue his studies for the priesthood, she did not fail to point out that "the grace of even wishing to belong to God must come from Himself". At the same time, he must "be cautious, my dear, dear friend, how you damp or check that good gift, which should be cherished as the richest mercy". Nevertheless, she insisted that, for one on whom God has bestowed the grace of vocation, the priesthood has a spiritual security beyond all others: "A man may be a very good man in the pursuit of any other profession; but certainly that of a clergyman is the easiest, surest road to God"—she was taking a different tack than Egan, who actually felt the burdens of the priesthood—"and the first, the highest and most blessed that can adorn a Human Being—The Peace of God is the full, the sure and certain compensation for any discouragement or obstacles the world may throw in the way—and His guidance *and favor* till Death, in Death, and after Death, the reward and crown of him who faithfully served Him."[116]

Even as a Protestant, Elizabeth had hoped that at least one of her boys might be a devout servant of the Lord as was her adored Henry Hobart. When William was only five, Elizabeth told Rebecca Seton how "Bill called out, as he opened his eyes this morning, 'Dear Henry Hubbard, I wish you would preach for me.' Just those words. They woke me from my sleep and occasioned a long, heavy sigh . . . the anxious presage and hope, that He might teach the wisher to be a preacher—oh, what a thought!"[117] At Emmitsburg she rejoiced to see both William and Richard serving Mass. "To have seen my own two boys in the sanctuary this day", she once exclaimed to Bruté, "at the moment of the elevation, each holding the chasuble—then Communion! What is the heart made of, to hold so much?"[118] The sanctuary was not, however, to be their home, and it was one of her private griefs. "He sees the torrents [of tears] at the thought that I bore and suckled them for anything but His service", she confided to Bruté. "Oh, do, do pray."[119]

This grief surfaced anew when a chance meeting with a former seminarian set off a passionate lament for the thin ranks of the priesthood. "May you be spared the agony of heart", Elizabeth cried out to Bruté,

> to see the poor, good *Lipp,* who once adorned your sanctuary in Baltimore where I had last seen him, now with wife and child. I burst in tears to Our Jesus redoubled. Oh, His Kingdom! Laborers for His vineyard! My poor, poor, poor Richard, William—My God, oh if the bleeding of a mother's heart can obtain! Poor, poor, poor blind ones! Such a Lord! Such a Master! Such a divine and glorious service!—but blind, blind, and lost to love and duty, groping alone through the bright, heavenly light which shines so lovely to the happy ones who *comprehend.* Blessed, blessed G., most blessed, you are *His* and in that, at least, [the] grateful soul of your own Mother rejoices. And, oh, remember those who are not.[120]

Those who persevered never forgot the part Elizabeth played in their perseverance. Thus, William Gellespie asked John Hickey to "give my respects to Mother Seton when you see her again; tell her to pray for her son as she kindly used to call me".[121] And Egan confided to William Seton: "I often imagine I see . . . our Dearest Mother looking down on us here below and afflicted when we do wrong—rejoicing when we do well and praying hard for us to obtain a seat [in heaven]."[122]

St. Elizabeth Ann's awe for the office of the priest goaded her to its defense when she saw priests of her acquaintance take it lightly, as in her sharp rebuke to John Hickey when he had preached badly.[123] Indeed, her anguish at their shortcomings compelled her, as Bruté once suggested: "O that priests felt for themselves as Mother Seton felt they ought to be! How much did she not suffer in witnessing their imperfections! How sorrowfully yet how charitably did she consider their faults!"[124] She took a special interest in Hickey, whom she had known from the time he was a student at the Mount, and counted him as a friend and correspondent. For these reasons her advice to him was as frank as it was wise, and surely it made him a better priest. When he had been sententious in rebuking his sister, who was a pupil at St. Joseph's, Elizabeth told him bluntly:

> I do not like . . . some things you wrote Ellen lately. You and I speak all through eternity; but take advice from your old Mother—I am a hundred to your thirty in experience, that cruel friend of our earthly journey.
>
> When you ask too much at first, you often gain nothing at last. *And if the heart is lost, all is lost.* If you use such language to your family, they cannot love you, since they have not our microscopes to see things as they are. Your austere, hard language was not understood by Ellen who, dear soul, considers your letters as mere curiosity. She loves and venerates you, but do not push her away. . . . Gently, gently, my father in God and son in heart.

Then the swift larger, telling question: "Do you drive so in the tribunal? I hope not.

"The faults of young people, especially such faults as Elinor's," Elizabeth explained patiently, "must be moved by prayer and tears, because they are *constitutional* and cannot be frightened out. I have said much harder things to her than you do, but turning the tune in her own heart, and not"—here she could not forego derision—"her poor, dear family quite as respectable even—as to the point you press on so valiantly—as half our Legislature, Senate, etc. How can you, in such a country as ours, dwell on such a motive of humility?"[125]

Another time, Elizabeth spiritedly defended Hickey's brother William, a student at the Mount, again contrasting the privileged graces the priest had received from God's hand: "William is surely one of the most estimable young men of the world. What a precious diamond, to be so covered with the cares of this world! But how can he help it? Be you gentle and considerate to him," she warned, "you blessed man of God, feeding on sweetmeats every morning and rejoicing your heart with the choicest wine. Had his disposition to virtue and religion been cultivated as yours has been," she finished mischievously, "he would be already your equal, I believe—but not sure."[126]

The one with whom Elizabeth shared most deeply her passionate love for Christ's priesthood was, naturally, her closest priest-friend, Father Simon Gabriel Bruté. In a very true sense, they directed each other's souls in an intimate sharing of their intense love for God. Frequently, in fact, she assumed the natural role of mother, for he was young and new to America. It was she who largely taught him the difficult language of his adopted land—she had spoken his native French from childhood—with *The Imitation of Christ* for his textbook, taking him through it laboriously and patiently, line by line, sentence by sentence. It was she, also, who unlocked for others his beautiful concepts of God's love by giving them full-blown expansion in the sentences and paragraphs he could not yet write; but he, for his part, did not shirk the ordeal of preaching them, "bad preaching as it may be", ignoring humbly the half-stifled smiles at mispronunciations and awkward choice of words, for it was his solemn calling as well as the only practical way, he admitted, "to force this dreadful English into my backward head".[127]

When Bruté was summoned to the Sulpician motherhouse in Paris, Mother Seton made sure the recognition would not go to his head. "Mr. Tessier writes in such triumph that his darling was called for even by the superior overseas *on particular business*", she teased, "and how happy that thy precious pearl was esteemed and confided in equally by *both*. The clearer eye of the Mountain [Father Dubois] and old microscope of the Valley [herself] must laugh at these doting grandpapas, though so venerable. The darling himself must smile at their poor, blind optics. Our Lord permits; let it pass. *Tu es sacerdos in aeternum secundum ordinem Melchisedech.* There the soul's grand triumph—all else but smoke."[128]

Whatever Bruté's business in Paris, the recognition by his superiors in Baltimore and Paris was deserved. The old and ailing Father Duhamel attested to it in his grumbling way as Elizabeth, highly amused, reported to Bruté: "Poor Hickey got a great compliment this morning", the old man had told her.

An Irishman told him the three priests at the Mountain all put
together are not worth one Bruté. Poor creatures, they tell me to
my face—now Bruté's gone, all is gone! Some say they will not
go to confession till he comes again. Poor, dear, good Bruté! Did
you see his letter, Ma'am, *to everybody* to *save souls?* Poor, crazy
Bruté! He says he will be on the high seas—he would be much
better *here,* attending his congregation. He could tend six con-
gregations at least. He can do what would kill ten men, if you
only give him bread, and two or three horses to ride to death,
one after t'other. Poor gentleman, if he was but steady![129]

There is no mistaking Elizabeth's affection and trust shining through
her amusement. In fact, she put it plainly in recounting for the
traveler, with the same mischievous delight, Father Dubois' retreat
for her pupils: "Almost I laughed out at his opening, telling
[them] . . . to be as many little stumps—no, *'chunks'*—of fire put
together. *One,* he said, if left *alone,* would soon go out. My eye
fell on an old black stump in the corner [herself]—and a big,
inward sigh to the live coal far away which used to give us the
blaze in a moment."[130]

Elizabeth's underlying sorrow at this long separation from her
soul's father and friend was renewed when, shortly after her
return, he was off again to Baltimore to take over new duties as
President of St. Mary's College. There was no teasing this time.
"In this little life of your Mother, not a moment since I saw you to
write a word but the meditation," she lamented,

or a volume would not have been enough to say half the heart
that fastens to yours more and more, if possible—but with such
freedom of the local circumstance, or position of the moment,
that I shall see you go again to fulfill your big *Presidentship* (oh,
bad omen, G., I did not know that tear was there)—Well, I will
see you go to do *His Will of the present moment* with no other
sighs or desires but for its most full and complete *accomplishment.*
Your little silly woman in the fields (most happy name and
place for her, my G.) your little woman, silly of our dear silliness
of prayers and tears, will now hold closer and closer to *Him* who
will do *all in you,* as He does in my poor little daily part, and

try always to bring you (*tut!* there again my candle is so dim I cannot see) ... try always every moment to bring you the support of a Mother's prayers, her cry to Him for your full fidelity as for our poor William's deliverance from *evil.*[131]

The teasing spirit that disguised so much love and wisdom returned in a dialogue between "Sam"—the name Elizabeth inveterately applied to the devil—and Bruté's "Good Angel":

Sam—now we'll catch *M. le President!* First, we will fill his head with plans of reformation—every successor improves his predecessor, to be sure! Of course, with the *succession* comes multiplied distractions of thought, complaisances, etc.—that alone a fine trap, if there was no other, but (oh, joy to the grinner!) we will catch him, too, by endless conversations and opinions (to be sure, a president must be *full* of opinions!).

This seraphim's wings shall be clipped; and the modest, retiring, devout spirit shall swell and fill and push and insist (oh, be joyful, what a change we will see!) and this simple heart, loving now to see but his God in, and the salvation of, souls, shall be plunged in the labyrinths of science and grow fat as a doctor (oh, we will have fun this next year, 1816!)—short thanksgivings, quick preparations, forced offerings. ...

"Good Angel"—Well, at least he will have abundant sacrifice of dearest, choicest consolations. He will act in full opposition to his own choice. His daily bread will be dry and hard. He will be a bond of union and peace to his confreres, a *spirit* of purest, ardent piety to worldlings, and an example of cheerful and tender forbearance to his pupils—poor, dear G., after a little while of subjection and patience to his wild heart, it *shall* be set free from the yoke, improved and experienced, to return with new ardor to its more simple and heavenly delights.[132]

Unquestionably, Elizabeth viewed Bruté's new appointment as curious and mistaken, for he is certainly the second person contrasted in the following comment on the vagaries too often encountered in the religious life: "While I say our *Te Deum* in union with your thanksgiving, my heart fills at 'O Lord, save Thy people,' thinking how things are shared in this world", she confided to him. "I see

a quiet, moderate, *experienced* man put in the center of a congregation who is not 'saved' for want of an active, zealous, driving man,
because they must have 'fire' cried in their ears; and I see a zealous,
driving man without *experience* put in a seminary where he will
'*save*' none, because he cannot wait to gain a heart or unfold a
temper, and his goal, instead of bedewing the plant in the thirsty
ground, crushes it under foot. Alas, well if he does not root it out
forever!" That her comments were comments and nothing more,
neither resentment nor criticism and certainly not a quarrel with
God, is evident in the close: "O Lord, then '*save!*' Save the
redeemed of Thy Precious Blood, and send wisdom from above.
'Blessed,' I am truly *downhearted* this day, poor leper! Yet, 'Glory
to the Father, Son and Holy Ghost!' has been my incessant prayer
with one hundred meanings. Too sick to do anything but pray."[133]

Much as Elizabeth admired the "active, zealous, driving man"
in Bruté, she knew from experience of her own nature that the
holiest zeal had at times to be tamed. It was indeed the exuberance
of both their souls that made them such a unique pair in God. She
had once confided to him that it would be

> like changing an Ethiopian to pretend to preserve the spirit of
> detail which the charity and natural disposition of our Superior
> [Father Dubois] has made the spirit of our community. Long
> may Our Lord spare him to it, for who could ever be found to
> *unwind the ball* as he does, and stop to pick out every knot? Too
> happy I to break the knot and piece it again! And it does seem to
> blind eyes like mine, so far from the spirit of simplicity to be
> obliged to spell every word and feel the pulse with *your Sisters,*
> but I will try more and more.[134]

Elizabeth did not hesitate, then, to bring her beloved priest-
director-son up short when nature overstepped its bounds, resulting
in runaway enthusiasm or foolish sensitivity. "My Blessed, all is a
true mystery to me in your disposition, much greater than any of
Faith", she once lectured him sharply.

> A man of your particular principle *on paper,* who has evidently
> the most dear and special graces—not given drop by drop as to

other souls, but poured over your head in a daily torrent—yet I seldom see you but in such wild enthusiasm of your own impression of the moment that you can see nothing, hear nothing, but that one object; or else quite *reserved, hurt* and *anxious* because you have not been consulted in things *which spoke for themselves,* or others which we would not dare take your advice about without knowing the Superior's will, or others again which, like the poor German smiths, we go over in our blind ignorance and I never even guess I have not done well till someone points it out.

How troubled, too, because Mr. Dubois doesn't come, and what responsibility have you? Is it your zeal and desire of the good you imagine he will do?

Elizabeth asked pointedly, and then got down to the points of practical administration with which, she strongly hinted, Bruté was familiar: "You ought to know our Reverend Superior by this time and see that he is not to be pushed anywhere; and your urging cannot but keep him away. When anything *essential* happens, I always inform him of it; and if the thing is not essential, his absence often hinders a fuss about nothing, and suffers little pets and passions to drop in silence. You speak as if your Mother's confidence is deficient, but it is surely not at this time I am to open your eyes to my situation in this community."[135] While the good man must have been properly chastened after such a relentless scolding, he must at the same time have been humbler and wiser, which was his "Mother's" whole purpose.

In the final months of St. Elizabeth Ann's life, the fires of that deeply spiritual friendship that had warmed the hearts of Bruté and herself in its lighthearted familiarity and humor on her part— she knew no other way with her friends—and the sacred lights and flashes of mysticism it ignited in both were deliberately banked by mutual consent as a final sacrifice of purification. "We have broken our old bonds", she told John Hickey. "I seldom speak to him but in the tribunal. What a lofty grace for this low earth!—but it is to be nearer in heaven, I hope."[136]

Elizabeth spelled out their motivation by indirection in a subsequent letter to Hickey, who wanted to return to Mount St. Mary's from Baltimore:

> My heart and soul this week past has been *under the press* of the Beatitude: "Blessed are the pure of heart—they shall see God." . . . Happy, happy are you to live all for Him. Every bent of your heart's affection, every power of your soul, turned wholly to Him without even the mixture of the innocent sojourning with your old father [Dubois] and dear brother [Bruté]. How much purer is your service where you are above the midst of earthly attraction. One thing I hope you are convinced of (I as a wretched sinner know it well), that wherever we meet a little prop of human comfort, there is always some subtraction of divine comfort. For my part, I am so afraid to cause any such subtraction, that I feel a reserve and fear in every human consolation that makes them more my pains than my pleasure.

She was not, however, pressing such difficult sublimity on others: "Yet the liberty of the children of God I hope in all. I only mean to say we should be too happy when the Providence of God keeps us wholly to Himself."[137]

The saint once gave definitive tongue to the ardent apostolic spirit that fueled her life and works in an ecstatic response to Bruté's thoughts of going with Father Samuel Cooper to preach the gospel to the Canadian Indians. "Blessed, your poor little *Bête*-Mother is lost these days past in your Canada letters", she began.

> Oh my! To see man a wild savage, a polished savage, man in any state what a savage!—unless he be in Christ. Oh, Blessed, I gasp with the desires to Him whom you are now carrying in and on your breast for full, whole accomplishment of His blessed Will. I glance a fearful look at you and Mr. Cooper and say secretly: if I was one or the other! Then adore and think. I know nothing about it; it only seems to me that those who have light and grace already might be trusted to keep it: and I would not stop night or day until I reached the dry and dark wilderness where neither can be found, where such horrid crimes go on for want of them, and where there is such a glorious death to be gained by carrying

them. O, G., if I was light and life as you are, I would shout like a madman alone to my God, and roar and groan and sigh and be silent all together until I had baptized a thousand and snatched these poor victims from hell.

There can be no doubting the sincerity and depths of Elizabeth's desire, for she turned immediately and honestly to her everyday calling:

And pray, *Madame Bête,* say you, why does not your zeal make its flame through its own little hemisphere? True—but rules, prudence, subjections, opinions, etc.—dreadful walls to a burning soul wild as mine and *somebody's....* I am like a fiery horse I had when a girl, whom they tried to break by making him drag a heavy cart; and the poor beast was so humbled that he could never more be inspired by whip or caresses, and wasted to a skeleton until he died. But you and Mr. Cooper might waste to skeletons to some purpose, and after wasting be sent loving to the glories of the Kingdom.

In the meantime, that Kingdom come. Every day I ask my *bête*-soul what I do for it in my little part assigned, and I can see nothing but the smile, caress, be patient, write, pray and WAIT before Him. O, G., G., G., my blessed God, that Kingdom come![138]

8

"MY BLESSED FAITH"

The mystery of the Church was the central fact and factor of St. Elizabeth Ann Seton's life and holiness. Without it she never would have lived the fullness of her apostolic life, reached the pinnacle of sanctity and perfection, or been hailed by that same Church in the loving gesture of canonization.

Elizabeth was not born into the totality of the mystery that, the Fathers of Vatican II confirmed, "subsists in the Catholic Church".[1] Rather, she was the heir of "many elements of sanctification and of truth . . . found outside of its visible structure"[2] in her native Episcopal church, but she was thankfully to become a memorable witness that "these elements, as gifts belonging to the Church of Christ, are forces impelling toward Catholic unity".[3] Pope Paul VI paid tribute to their unifying power in thanking the Episcopal church for the gift of Elizabeth Seton. "To this Church goes the merit of having awakened and fostered the religious sense and Christian sentiment which in the young Elizabeth were naturally predisposed to the most spontaneous and lively manifestations", he acknowledged. "We willingly recognize this merit, and, knowing well how much it cost Elizabeth to pass over to the Catholic Church, we admire her courage for adhering to the religious truth and divine reality which were manifested to her therein. And we are likewise pleased to see that from this same adherence to the Catholic Church she experienced great peace and security", a soundness of soul that caused her to find "it natural to preserve all

the good things which her membership in the fervent Episcopalian community had taught her, in so many beautiful expressions,
especially of religious piety, and that she was always faithful in her
esteem and affection for those from whom her Catholic profession had sadly separated her".[4] And the Holy Father finished by
noting in the official presence of Episcopalian prelates and digni-
taries "a motive of hope and a presage of ever better ecumenical
relations".[5]

Among Elizabeth's writings there is, whether from her own
thoughts or from some book, a short, sensible treatment of mystery:
"When we say this thing is a mystery, of the *thing* we say nothing,
but of ourselves we say that we do not comprehend this thing—as
defect of strength in us makes some weights to be immobile, so likewise defect of understanding makes some truths to be mysterious."[6]
Before she ever confronted the mystery of the Church, she stumbled
upon a lesser but nonetheless obstructive mystery, something she
did not comprehend because she had never even considered it, the
possibility that there was only one true Church, or even that any
church was truly necessary. She had always taken for granted that
"everybody would be saved who meant well".[7] As she explained
to Father Bruté years later when he made an attempt to convert
her sister, Mary Post: "Your letter to Sister admirable, if first the
big stone of darkest ignorance and indifference was removed on
the point of first necessity—*that there is any true or false Church,
right faith or wrong faith.* But, blessed Soul, [neither] you, nor
anyone who has not been in that ignorance or indifference, can
imagine the size and depth of it." She tried to make him see that,
secure in the Church as she was now, she had once been as adrift
and heedless as Mary Post:

> And putting myself again a moment in the place of my sister
> (even with my great advantage of having been passionately
> attached to religion when a Protestant, which she is not), I
> imagine I read your letter and, looking up with vacant surprise
> would say:
>   "What does the man mean? Would he say that all who believe
> in Our Lord are not safe, or even if a poor Turk or savage does

not believe, is he to be blamed for it? They make God a merciful Being indeed, if He would condemn souls of His own creation for their parents bringing them in the world on one side of it or the other."[8]

Eliza Sadler had also been the target of Bruté's zeal. She was not in the least offended; rather, she praised his kind thought of her and devotion to his duty, but her answer was exactly what Elizabeth could have predicted: "The truth, however, obliges me", Mrs. Sadler told Bruté, "to assure you that I feel it impossible to subscribe to the belief that out of your Church there can be no Christians. Ever since I have been capable of reason, I have endeavored humbly to make the law of my Redeemer the rule and guide of my actions, unworthily and imperfectly, but not blindly; and I believe that *He* who sees the inmost thoughts will judge of my faith, as He promised to do by all those who believe in His Name."[9]

Elizabeth further buttressed her opinion of the fruitlessness of Bruté's attempts with the example of her brother-in-law, Dr. Wright Post, who

> once asked me so simply:
> "Sister Seton, they say you go to the Catholic Church. What is the difference?"
> *"It is the first Church, my brother, the old Church, the Apostles begun"* (answered the poor, trembling Betsy Seton, dreading always to be pushed on the subject she could only feel, but never express to these coolest reasoners).
> *"Church of the Apostles"*, said my brother, "Why, is not every church from the apostles?"[10]

Speak as she might of "cool reasoners", Elizabeth seemed to insist in the end that the ignorance she once shared had really little to do with reason or arguments. "For, ever accustomed to look only to little exterior attractions", she explained, "as the dress and quiet of the Quakers, a sweet, enthusiastic preaching among the Methodists, a soft, melting music of low voices among Anabaptists, or any other such nonsense, the thought of a right faith or wrong faith, true church or false one, never enters the mind of one among a hundred."[11]

Amusingly enough, Bruté, for his part, failed to understand Elizabeth's attitude or exposition, for he wrote across the head of this letter: "A letter to try to convert Mrs. Post, her sister, to the Catholic faith—how useless she thought it—most curious."[12]

Certainly Elizabeth had no least thought of one true Church when she met the Filicchis in Livorno, Italy. It was her evident piety—passing acquaintances had already judged that "if she was not a heretic, she would be a saint"[13]—that prompted the Filicchi brothers to acquaint her with the Catholic claims almost as soon as she arrived among them. "May the good Almighty God enlighten your mind and strengthen your heart to see and follow in religion the surest, true way to the eternal blessings",[14] Antonio prayed. Filippo more bluntly informed her of her obligation to seek the truth. She tried to pass it off with banter: "Oh, my, sir, if there is but one Faith, and nobody pleases God without it, where are all the good people who die out of it?" Filippo was not to be deterred: "I don't know", he answered frankly. "That depends on what light of Faith they had received. But I know where people go who can know the right Faith, if they pray for it and inquire for it, and yet do neither." Nothing could be blunter than that, with its affirmation of the grace God was extending her and the dire results of its rejection.

Whether from embarrassment or unease or even fright, Elizabeth tried to maintain lightness of tone: "Much as to say, sir, you want me to pray and inquire, and be of your Faith?" "Pray and inquire, that is all I ask", was the unmoving reply.[15] It was an important conversation—the fact that Elizabeth recorded it word for word for Rebecca Seton attests to that—and Filippo had found his mark: Elizabeth did set out seriously on the long, painful road of prayer and inquiry, however lightheartedly she attempted to describe it for Rebecca: "So, dearest Bec, I am laughing with God when I try to be serious and say daily, as the good gentleman told me, in old Mr. Pope's words: *'If I am wrong, Thy grace impart to find the better way.'* Not that I can think there is a better way than I know—but every one must be respected in their own."[16]

Elizabeth's earnest and prayerful seeking was furthered and sweetened by her immediate attraction to certain Catholic teachings and practices, such as the day-long availability of the churches for private prayer, the belief in the Real Presence of Christ in these same churches, devotion to the Blessed Virgin, fasting and penance.[17] But the uncompromising fact of a single true Faith and its consequences did not confront her until, at her minister Henry Hobart's request, she had read Thomas Newton's *Dissertation of the Prophecies*. She had felt, perhaps, that if her inquiries led nowhere, she could always retreat to the haven of her native Episcopal church. Now she realized that this was not so. "It grieves my very soul", she cried out to Amabilia Filicchi, "to see that Protestants as well as your (as I thought, hard and severe) principles see the thing so differently; since this book so valued by them sends all followers of the Pope to the bottomless Pit"—and she finished ruefully, her eye on the first millennium and a half of Christendom—"it appears by the account made of them from the Apostles' time, that a greater part of the world must be already there, at that rate."[18]

There was no turning back, and Elizabeth pushed on bravely. When Hobart asked her, "What more would you have when you act according to your best judgment?" she answered that her judgment would be enough for this world, "but I fear in the next to meet *another* question".[19]

Throughout the bitterness of the struggle, which eventually frayed Elizabeth's nerves and physically reduced her almost to a skeleton, she never let go of her confidence in God. She besought Him "to enlighten me to see the truth unmixed with doubts and hesitations. I read the promises given to St. Peter and the Sixth Chapter [of St.] John every day", she assured Antonio Filicchi, "and then ask God, can I offend Him by believing those express words?"

The sense and authority of Scripture were very strong in Elizabeth. "I read my *dear St. Francis,* and ask if it is possible that I shall dare to think differently from him, or seek heaven any other way. I have read your *England's Reformation,* and find its evidence too conclusive to admit of any reply. God will not forsake me, Antonio. I know that He will unite me to His flock; and, although now my Faith is unsettled, I am assured that He will not disappoint my hope which is fixed on His own word, that He will not despise the humble, contrite heart."[20]

How unerringly this sincere but sorely tried and confused woman penetrated the mystery of the Church's lowliness! A century and a half later, the Fathers of Vatican II were to expound these very virtues of the Church that she possesses in imitation of her Master and Head: "Just as Christ carried out the work of redemption in poverty and persecution, so the Church is called to follow the same route that it might communicate the fruits of salvation to men. Christ Jesus, 'though He was by nature God . . . emptied Himself, taking the nature of a slave,'[21] and 'being rich, became poor,'[22] for our sakes. Thus, the Church, although it needs human resources to carry out its mission, is not set up to seek earthly glory, but to proclaim, even by its own example, humility and self-sacrifice." The Fathers, too, were to confirm the rightness of Elizabeth's trust: "Christ was sent by the Father 'to bring good news to the poor, to heal the contrite of heart'."[23]

Despite Elizabeth's striving for complete self-honesty and disinterestedness, the struggle to the truth was so long and bitter that Bishop Carroll warned that, even so, she "ought to consider whether the tears she sheds and the prayers she offers to heaven are purely for God's sake and arise solely from compunction for sin, and are unmixed with any alloy of worldly respect or inordinate solicitude for the attainment of some worldly purpose. . . . A fear arises in my mind that God discovers in her some lurking imperfection, and defers the final grace of her conversion till her soul be entirely purified of its irregular attachments."[24] The Bishop's fears were surely justified, for without his being fully aware of it he seems to have sensed that this was a struggle for a great and unusual soul. Indeed, Elizabeth's own accounts of her anguish bore out the justice of his uneasiness, for no matter what she did to attain truth and peace, she was rebuffed again and again; her exertions brought only further confusion and darkness.

"I fell on my face before God (remember I tell you all)", Elizabeth confessed to Antonio Filicchi,

> and appealed to Him as my righteous Judge, if hardness of heart, or unwillingness to be taught or any human reasons, stood between me and the truth; if I would not rejoice to cast my sorrows in the bosom of the Blessed Mary, to entreat the influence of all His blessed saints and angels, to pray for precious souls even more than for myself, and account myself happy in dying for His sacred truth—if once my soul could know it was pleasing to Him. I remembered how much these exercises had comforted and delighted me at Leghorn, and recalled all the reasons which had then convinced me of their truth—and immediately a cloud of doubts and replies raised a contest in this poor soul, and I could only cry out for mercy to a sinner.[25]

Although Antonio and his brother Filippo continued faithful in writing Elizabeth long, encouraging letters, they also unwittingly added to her confusion—she was being pushed and pulled by friends on both sides—and Filippo at length gave her what was probably the best advice of all. "Avoid the labyrinth of controversies", he wrote. "They will not make you wiser."[26] Even the best advice, however, does not always work out in practice, as Elizabeth discovered:

> After reading the life of St. Mary Magdalen, I thought: "Come, my soul, let us turn from all these suggestions of one side or the other, and quietly resolve to go to that church which has at least the multitude of the wise and good on its side"; and began to consider the first step I must take. The first step—is it not to declare I believe all that is taught by the Council of Trent?—and if I said that, would not the Searcher of Hearts know my falsehood and insincerity? Could you say that you would be satisfied with His bread and believe the cup, which He equally commanded, unnecessary?[*] Could you believe that the prayers and litanies addressed to Our Blessed Lady were acceptable to God, though not commanded in Scripture, etc., etc.?[27]

[*] Only in recent years has the Catholic Church resumed Communion under both species.

Elizabeth knew the root cause of her trouble better than anyone: "Far different is my situation from those who are uninstructed," she told Antonio, "but my hard case is to have a head turned with instruction, without the light in my soul to direct it where to rest."[28]

In the end, the long sought and prayed-for light flooded Elizabeth's soul in God's gift and stilled the turmoil of controversy and doubt. "I WILL GO PEACEABLY AND FIRMLY TO THE CATHOLIC CHURCH: for if Faith is so important to our salvation, I will seek it where true Faith first began, seek it among those who received it from GOD HIMSELF", she announced resolutely to Amabilia Filicchi. "The controversies on it I am quite incapable of deciding; and as the strictest Protestant allows salvation to a good Catholic, to the Catholics I will go and try to be a good one. May God accept my intention and pity me."[29]

Elizabeth saw now clearly what Filippo meant, that faith, not conviction, was the key, that faith was all that was required. "I tell you a secret hidden almost from my own soul, it is so delicate," she confessed to Gabriel Bruté many years later,

> THAT my hatred of opposition, troublesome inquiries, etc. brought me in the CHURCH more than CONVICTION—how often I argued to my fearful, uncertain heart, at all events CATHOLICS must be as safe as any other religion; they say none are safe but themselves—*perhaps it is true.* If not, at all events I shall be safe with them as any other—it is the way of suffering and the cross for me that is another point of security . . . there, dearest G, you read what I would have carried to the grave, only I wish you to know well, as far as I can tell you, the impossibility for a poor Protestant to see our meaning without being led step by step and the veil lifted little by little—I am cold to my bone, and hand and heart trembling while I think how I have passed through the thousand mazes—and my thousand ifs to Our God, yet appealing to Him *the if* was only fear to displease Him."[30]

The mazes were gone and the ifs forgotten on March 14, 1805, when, in the presence of Father Matthew O'Brien and Antonio Filicchi, Elizabeth united herself fully to the one true Church of Jesus Christ. Father, later Bishop, Cheverus of Boston had given her the final push. "The doubts which arise in your mind do not destroy your faith; they only disturb your mind", he had assured her. "Who in this life, my dear Madam, is perfectly free from such troubles? 'We see as through a glass in an obscure manner,' we stand like Israelites at the foot of the holy mountain, but in spite of dark clouds and the noise of thunder, we perceive some rays of the glory of the Lord, and we hear His divine Voice. I would, therefore, advise your joining the Catholic Church as soon as possible, and when doubts arise, say only: 'I believe, O Lord, help Thou my unbelief.' "[31]

While the word *Magisterium* was probably unknown to Elizabeth, now, ten days after Cheverus' welcome urging, Elizabeth penetrated with grace into the mystery of the Church's infallibility and not only freely accepted but also proclaimed her teaching authority. "After all were gone, I was called to the little room next the altar", she wrote happily to Amabilia Filicchi, "and there professed to believe what the *Council of Trent* believes and teaches; laughing with my heart to my Savior, who saw that I knew not what the Council of Trent believed—only that it believed what the Church of God declared to be its belief, and consequently is now *my belief.*"[32]

There is not the slightest doubt that by this act Elizabeth was embracing that "one Church of Christ which in the Creed is professed as one, holy, Catholic and apostolic, which our Savior after His Resurrection, commissioned Peter to shepherd, and him and the other apostles to extend and direct with authority, which He erected for all ages, as 'The pillar and mainstay of the truth.' This Church constituted and organized in the world as a society, subsists in the Catholic Church, which is governed by the successor of Peter and by the Bishops in communion with him."[33]

From the first Elizabeth was an "adorer ... of the mystery of *The Church,* the only ark in *the world*".[34] Once she had entered that ark, she gave it her unstinted loyalty and submission. Her respect for hierarchy, the ordered succession of superiors placed over her by God—pastor, spiritual director, religious superior, bishop, Pope—was untrammeled by self. As a new Catholic, she found that "the counsel and excellent directions of [Father] O'B[rien]...strengthen me and, being sometimes enforced by command, give a determination to my actions which is now indispensable".[35]

For the remaining years of her life she found the same guidance and ascetical surety in the succeeding spiritual directors sent her by God, and she so taught her religious daughters. "What was the first role of our dear Savior's life?" she asked in a conference. "You know it was to do His Father's Will....I know what His Will is by those who direct me; whatever they bid me do, if it is ever so small in itself, is the Will of God for me."[36]

Elizabeth had immediate joy, too, in the sacramental life of the Church. Although she was introduced to Catholic ceremonies in the unusual rites of Holy Week and was completely mystified, the veil was lifted whenever she discerned the structure of "the Divine Sacrifice, so commanding and yet already so familiar for all my wants and necessities. That speaks for itself, and I am all at home in it."[37] She was, of course, even more at home, from her Protestant days of preparation, with the holy Eucharist, for whose first reception she counted "the days and hours";[38] and it became, as it was intended, an instant source of strength in resisting the indignation of family and friends at her conversion. "From circumstances of peculiar impressions on my mind", she told Antonio, "I have been obliged to watch it so carefully and keep so near the Fountain Head, that I have been three times to communion since you left me, not to influence my faith, but to keep peace in my soul, which without this heavenly resource would be agitated and discomposed by the frequent assaults which, in my immediate situation, are naturally made on my feelings."[39]

Most striking of all was Elizabeth's reaching out for the sacrament of penance, a sacrament not always fully appreciated by native Catholics but of special discomfort and even fright to converts. Indeed, this sacrament played a decisive role in Elizabeth's final resolve to become a Catholic. On the fateful January Sunday in St. George's Church, at "the bowing of my heart before the [Episcopalian] Bishop to receive his absolution—which is given publicly and universally to all in the church—I had not the least faith in his prayer, and looked for an apostolic loosing from my sins, which by the books Mr. H[obart] had given me to read, I find they do not claim or admit."[40] How different her eager awaiting of the Catholic sacrament: "So delighted now to prepare for this good confession which, bad as I am, I would be ready to make on the housetop to insure the good *absolution* I hope for, after it."[41]

When Elizabeth made her first confession on March 20, 1805, it was an act of joy and remarkable for her instant perception of Christ in the sacrament. "It is done!" she exclaimed to Amabilia. "Easy enough: the kindest, most respectable confessor is this Mr. O'[Brien], with the compassion and yet firmness in this work of mercy which I would have expected from Our Lord Himself. Our Lord Himself I saw in him, both in his and my part of this venerable Sacrament, for, oh, Amabilia, how awful those words of unloosing after thirty years bondage! I felt as if my chains fell, as those of St. Peter at the touch of the divine Messenger. My God, what new scenes for my soul!"[42]

The following year Elizabeth was firmly and forever established in the full strength of the Church when Bishop John Carroll came to New York and, after a week of personal instructions and spiritual direction, confirmed her on Pentecost Sunday, May 26, 1806. She chose the confirmation name of Mary, which, she told Antonio contentedly, "added . . . to the *Ann Elizabeth* . . . present the three most endearing ideas in the world, and contain the memento of the mysteries of salvation".[43] The only sacrament proper to her and yet to be received was the sacrament of extreme unction, now called the sacrament of the sick. When Bruté administered the sacrament on September 24, 1820—it was repeated on January 2, 1821—he noted, "Mother so calm, so recollected and so wholly united to her Blessed Lord. Her eyes so expressive, the look that pierces heaven and the soul visible in it."[44]

There is no evidence that Elizabeth was rebaptized, that is, baptized conditionally, in the Catholic Church. Bishop Carroll and Bishop Cheverus both believed in the validity of Angelican baptism as then conferred, and in fact Carroll warned his priests against rebaptizing needlessly, citing penalties laid down by the Church for such acts.

In light of certain erroneous and even presumptuous opinions concerning the Church since Vatican II, it would be well to explore what the Church meant to St. Elizabeth Ann. Despite the Council's explicit teaching to the contrary, two important misconceptions are prevalent: the first, that the Church and the "institutional" Church are somehow distinct and different; the second, that being recognized as the People of God somehow allows members of the Church to proclaim, "We are the Church", in the sense of being on an equal footing with all other members, including the Pope and the hierarchy, in disregard of God-given charisms and authorities.

Concerning the first, Vatican II teaches that

> Christ, the one Mediator, established and continually sustains here on earth His holy Church, the community of faith, hope and charity, as an entity with visible delineation through which He communicated truth and grace to all. But, the society structured with hierarchical organs and the Mystical Body of Christ, are not to be considered as two realities, nor are the visible assembly and the spiritual community, nor the earthly Church and the Church enriched with heavenly things; rather they form one complex reality which coalesces from a divine and human element. For this reason, by no weak analogy, it is compared to the mystery of the Incarnate Word. As the assumed nature inseparably united to Him, serves the divine Word as a living organ of salvation, so, in a similar way, does the visible social structure of the Church serve the Spirit of Christ, who vivifies it, in the building up of the body.[45]

As for the second misconception, the Fathers of the Council surely acknowledge that "in the building up of Christ's Body various members and functions have their part to play". This is ordained by God: "There is only one Spirit who, according to His own richness and the needs of the ministries, gives His different gifts for the welfare of the Church." There is, however, a primacy of gifts: "What has a special place among these gifts is the grace of the Apostles to whose authority the Spirit Himself subjected even those who were endowed with charisms."[46] This grace and authority of the Apostles subsist in the Pope and the bishops in union with him.[47]

Another, no less essential, primacy of gifts is bestowed upon the ministerial priesthood shared by Pope, bishops and priests. "Though they differ from one another in essence and not only in degree, the common priesthood of the faithful and the ministerial or hierarchical priesthood are nonetheless interrelated: each of them in its own special way is a participation in the one priesthood of Christ", so teach the Fathers of Vatican II. "The ministerial priest, by the sacred power he enjoys, teaches and rules the priestly people; acting in the person of Christ, he makes present the Eucharistic Sacrifice, and offers it to God in the name of all the people. But the faithful, in virtue of their royal priesthood, join in the offering of the Eucharist. They likewise exercise that priesthood in receiving the sacraments, in prayer and thanksgiving, in the witness of a holy life, and by self-denial and active charity."[48] How well, from this definition, did Elizabeth Seton exercise her priesthood!

Even St. Thérèse of Lisieux, that lowliest of Christ's virgins who used the word "little" to describe everything she did and was, had problems with her place, her identity, in the Church. Having practically forced herself into the contemplative quiet of the cloister, she found herself besieged through her desire for divine and human service—not, be it noted, for power or influence—by a tumultuous desire for the missions and martyrdom, surely unrequitable where she was. "Since my longing for martyrdom was powerful and unsettling," she wrote, "I turned to the epistles of St. Paul in the hope of finally finding an answer. By chance the twelfth and thirteenth chapters of the first epistle to the Corinthians caught my attention, and in the first section I read that not everyone can be an apostle, prophet or teacher, that the Church is composed of a variety of members, and that the eye cannot be the hand"—it was in vain. "Even with such an answer revealed before me," she confessed, "I was not satisfied and did not find peace."

But: "I persevered in the reading and did not let my mind wander until I found this encouraging theme: 'Set your desires on the greater gifts. And I will now show you the way which surpasses all others.' For the Apostle insists that the greater gifts are nothing at all without love"—this made great sense to her, since love was her whole motivation—"and that this same love is surely the best path leading directly to God. At length I had found peace of mind.

"When I had looked upon the mystical body of the Church, I recognized myself in none of the members which St. Paul described," she admitted quite simply, "and what is more, I desired to distinguish myself more favorably within the whole body"—not certainly out of self-love but out of a sense of usefulness.

> Love appeared to me to be the hinge for my vocation. Indeed I knew that the Church had a body composed of various members, but in this body the necessary and more noble member was not lacking; I knew that the Church had a heart and that such a heart appeared to be aflame with love. I knew that one love drove the members of the Church to action, that if this love were extinguished, the apostles would have proclaimed the Gospel no longer, the martyrs would have shed their blood no more. I saw and realized that love sets off the bounds of all vocations

—how profound and satisfying to each member of the Mystical Body with his part divinely assigned!—

> that love is everything, that this same love embraces every time and every place. In one word, that love is everlasting.
>
> Then, nearly ecstatic with the supreme joy in my soul, I proclaimed: O Jesus, my love, at last I have found my calling: my call is love. Certainly I have found my proper place in the Church, and You gave me that very place, my God. In the heart of the Church, my mother, I will be love, and thus I will be all things, as my desire finds its direction.[49]

That same Church has assigned these words to be read in the divine office of St. Thérèse's feast day, because they say everything that is to be said about her.

There is a striking and humbling passage in St. Augustine vis-à-vis Our Lady and the Church. "The Virgin Mary is both holy and blessed, and yet the Church is greater than she", he writes. "Mary is a part of the Church, a member of the Church, a holy, an eminent—the most eminent—member, but still only a member of the entire body. The body undoubtedly is greater than she, one of its members. This body has the Lord for its head, and head and body together make up the whole Christ. In other words, our head is divine—our head is God."[50]

Elizabeth Seton's soul was docile and lowly before the mystery of the Church. It breathed forth gratitude when her days were running down. "I thank God for having made me a child of *His Church*", she wrote to a friend. "When you come to this hour, you *will know* what it is to be a child of the Church."[51] The use of the word *child* is significant. She was, in her own eyes, most gladly a child, with all the trust and dependence and utter love the word implies; she believed most fully that, as Jesus warned, unless she became as a little child, she would not enter the Kingdom of heaven. It was a usual word with her. When she felt that she had acted awkwardly or even wrongfully in the first days of the Sisterhood, she assured Bishop Carroll: "You will see how good a child I am going to be. Quite a little child. And perhaps you will have often to give me the food of little children yet, but I will do my best as I have promised you in every case."[52] On her deathbed, that great moment of farewell to her Sisters, she struggled mightily to pronounce the words that were her sacred legacy to them: "Be children of the Church, be children of the Church."[53]

Elizabeth had no difficulty in being "a sheep in the flock", which is what Father Bruté called her in praising the "reverence, tenderness, and interest she felt for her Superiors—for their holy life, for seeing them true priests". He added ruefully, "Ah! that priests felt for themselves as she felt they should be—how did she suffer even at their imperfections, at their faults how sorrowfully, yet how charitably."[54] She might naturally consider herself the center of the plans for the school and religious community she had been brought to Baltimore to found, but if she did so for a moment, she quickly corrected herself: "So much of my, or rather the *scheme* of these revered gentlemen", she told Antonio Filicchi, "depends on your concurrence and support that I dare not form a wish."[55] When the plans were reaching maturity, she avowed further that "if I had a choice, and my will would decide in a moment, I would remain silent in His hands".[56]

Elizabeth remained just as detached in spirit when the canonical establishment of the community was being readied. "The constitutions proposed have been discussed by our Reverend Director," she informed the Bishop, "and I find he makes some observations on my situation relative to them; but surely an individual is not to be considered where a public good is in question; and you know I would gladly make every sacrifice you think consistent with my first and inseparable obligations as a mother."[57] Although the director, Father John Dubois, had a temperament very different from Elizabeth's own, and his meticulousness annoyed her to the point that she sometimes made innocent fun of him with the Sisters, there was never a question of flouting him, either first as director or later as superior of the community. In fact, Elizabeth told Carroll that Dubois had always been her preference for superior because "being on the spot"—he lived up the road at Mount St. Mary's—"he sees things in a different point of view from those who are distant . . . and he always and invariably has recommended me to refer constantly to you, which is not only in the order of Providence, but the only safety I can find for the peace of my mind."[58]

The Bishop himself was, quite simply, "her father", and Elizabeth's obedience to him was unqualified. Even when she protested vehemently to him over what she rightfully considered usurpations of her community and school by the high-handed Father David, she could finish: "But if, after consideration of every circumstance, you still think things must remain as they are—whatever you dictate I will abide by through every difficulty."[59] When Carroll lay dying at eighty years of age, Elizabeth confided to a former pupil, "My eyes are blind with writing and tears. Our Blessed Archbishop's situation, tho' we must give and resign him, presses hard on me as well as on thousands, harder on me than you would imagine."[60]

Although the Pope, Pius VII, was a distant figure in a distant land, he was nonetheless an undeniable reality and rock of unity and truth. Elizabeth entered with a daughter's sorrow into his sufferings in Napoleon's prisons, making his prayer of submission to the Will of God her favorite prayer unto death.[61] Her first letter to Antonio Filicchi after the Emperor's final downfall began with her joy at "the glad and happy news of the restoration of Our Holy Father".[62] A tender sign of filial love was in a note to Napoleon's forlorn little nephew Jerome, a pupil at Mount St. Mary's, who had asked Mother Seton for an Agnus Dei "to preserve me in the vacations from the dangers that will surround me".[63] "Dear Jerome," she replied, "it is a great pleasure to me to send you the Agnus Dei. I wish I had one handsomely covered; but you will mind only the virtues of the prayers Our Holy Father has said over it."[64]

It is not to be thought that Elizabeth's submission to the Will of God as revealed through His Church and her ministers, a submission so profound that it was transformed into the purest love, as already noted, reduced her to being a kind of holy slave or automaton. To describe that lively, volatile, even passionate woman so could provoke only laughter. She once freely acknowledged that "rules, prudence, subjections, opinions, etc. 'were' dreadful walls to a burning soul wild as mine".[65] But those walls, freely entered, never really confined her. Her soul was more like the flag of her free country, whipping in the breeze. It was essentially a free soul, for truth had made it free; while firmly lashed to the pole of standard religious rules, it moved freely in the winds of the Spirit—the ardors, the enthusiasms, the spontaneous prayers and acts of devotion. Gabriel Bruté understood, because his own soul was so similar, and he gave Elizabeth's the space and air it needed. He even blew upon it with his own flashing, almost at times incoherent, spiritual cries and aspirations, then watched with satisfaction as it responded into leaping, straining life.

Elizabeth's joy in Bruté's understanding was unbounded: "Blessed G., I am so in love now with rules", she exulted, "that I see the *bit* of the bridle all gold, or the *reins* all of silk. You know my sincerity, since with the little attraction to your Brother's [Dubois'] government, I even eagerly seek the grace [of] the little cords he entangles me with."[66]

Over all was Elizabeth's whole-souled love of the Church: "All that I possess: *my blessed Faith*"[67] and its *"mysteries of love"*.[68] She set her calendar by its feast days, reveling in their beauty and feeding on their holiness: "Rogation days—the full cry of His whole Church!!!"[69] she once noted ardently, and again, "I *steal* to say litany of saints *for intention of the Church,* this blessed Ember Day."*[70] The Church has responded in kind, as Pope Paul declared, "before the Holy Catholic Church, before the entire American people, and before all humanity. Elizabeth Ann Bayley Seton is a saint. . . . The Church has exulted with admiration and joy, and has today heard her own charism of truth poured out in the exclamation that we send up to God and announce to the world: she is a saint."[71]

---

* Before the latest reform of the liturgy under Paul VI, the three days preceding Ascension Thursday were set aside as days of special prayer and were called rogation days (from the Latin *rogare,* to ask). Ember days of prayer and penance occurred four times a year.

9

"THE EMBRACE OF HIM WHO IS LOVE"

Death is still the greatest mystery of life, and it *is* a part of life, the most important part, its ending, its summing up, the irrevocable record of its success or failure. It quite naturally has a fascination for the living because of its very mystery. For the same reason it creates uneasiness ranging from wonder to terror. Faith enables the believer to penetrate the mystery in an essential way, but even faith cannot—or, in a sense, should not—dispel all fear and uncertainty.

"My grace is sufficient for you",[1] Jesus admonished St. Paul, and indeed His grace, so lovingly and lavishly given, transforms the worst aspects of death for those who love Him. It bestows its comforts in many ways. The waning of physical strength and weariness engendered by long years makes the thought of eternal rest in the Lord something to look forward to. Mother Seton felt this when she gently chided a former pupil: "I know your uneasiness for me, but that should not be. Why uneasy at the fulfillment of the merciful designs of so dear a Providence Who left me to take care of my *Bec,* to bring Jos to an age to take care of herself and our dearest boys to enter the way of life they were to choose . . . ? What would you have, darling? Why be anxious if your poor, tired friend goes to rest?—I HOPE!"[2] There is a similar thought among her notes for conferences to the Sisters: "Consider a good death as a call to the wedding feast of the Lamb—St. Gregory says it will not be a dinner banquet, *but a supper,* to be followed by

ETERNAL REST."[3] These last words in capitals are also underlined three times!

Nor is it unfounded to observe that the fear of death decreases in God's servants with the deepening of their love for Him over the years. A few privileged souls who have outdistanced all others in probing God's love and responding to it *yearn* for glorious eternal union with Him. Elizabeth Seton was such a one. The saintly Bishop Cheverus knew whereof he spoke when he told her: "I envy you, running now to the embrace of Him who is love."[4] And she herself called death "this dear, dearest thief".[5]

From earliest childhood Elizabeth's precocious piety softened the face of death for her. She recalled that at the age of four "they asked me: did I not cry when little Kitty was dead? No, because Kitty is gone up to heaven. I wish I could go, too, with Mama."[6] It is significant that as a child she chose for her favorite Psalm: "The Lord is my Shepherd, the Lord ruleth me . . . though I walk in the midst of the shadow of death, I will fear no evil, for Thou art with me."[7] It was only in mature years, with the comprehension of sin and its punishment, that the element of fear entered her soul, but it was a healthy, life-giving fear, except in the first awkward days of dawning holiness, for she knew it could be banished with sorrow, absolution, penance and trust.

Elizabeth had this fear all her life for loved ones, for her family and friends. The most poignant expression of her constant, nagging concern is in a letter to Julia Scott describing the deathbed of Elizabeth's sister-in-law Eliza Maitland. "Julia, my precious friend, this dear Eliza did not love the world", she wrote in pity.

> She had a bitter portion in it; and you would say a life passed in the slavery of poverty and secluded from those allurements which commonly endear us to the present scene would have ensured her at least a peaceful death. Some nights before her last, in an interval of ease, she conversed with me and observed herself that such had been her situation, but added: "How is it, that until we are just going, we never think of the necessary dispositions to meet death?" I made some consolatory reflections

to her; but, although she said but little on the subject during her illness . . . her fears and dread continued to the last.

Then a great cry:

Oh, Julia, Julia, Julia! "The last, last, last sad silence." The soul departing without hope. Its views, its interests centered in a world it is hurried from. No Father's sheltering arms, no heavenly Home of joy. My Julia, Julia, Julia! Eternity—a word of transport, or of agony. Your friend, your own, your true, your dear friend begs you, supplicates you, in the Name of GOD—think of it! Oh, if she should see your precious soul torn, dragged an unwilling victim—what a thought of horror![8]

It had long been commonplace for anyone who was sick or dying to send for Elizabeth to nurse them. Her most precious deathbed of all, her husband's, had raised this corporal work of mercy to a true divine discipleship. "When I thank God for my creation and preservation, it is with a warmth of feeling I never could know until now: to wait on *Him* in my William's soul and body," she had written exaltedly in the *lazaretto,*

to console and soothe those hours of affliction and pain, watching and weariness which, next to God, I alone could do, to strike up the cheerful notes of hope and Christian triumph, which from his partial love he hears with the more enjoyment from me, because to me he attributes the greatest share of them; to hear him, in pronouncing the name of his Redeemer, declare that I first taught him the sweetness of the sound—oh, if I was in the dungeon of this *lazaretto,* I should bless and praise my God for those days of retirement and abstraction from the world, which have afforded leisure and opportunity for so blessed a work.[9]

In Elizabeth's new life of religious service in the Church, her perception of assisting the dying as a sacred ministry reached the heights that were at the same time intimate and exalted. Despite the human grief and emotional suffering she endured in the long illnesses and wrenching deaths of her beloved daughters, there was a mystical happiness, the reward of her own ever-deepening understanding and holiness. Of Annina's last anointing she wrote with true joy: "The desire for the Holy Oil seemed almost to disturb her, but Our Dearest was so good as to hasten our wish." *Our* wish. Much of the joy was in the holy union forged by the mother and eagerly embraced by the pliant child. "The Reverend Superior arrived. What a moment for her! He must wait for a book, and she kept her eyes on a crucifix when the pouring sweat and agony of pain would permit. When it came, she presented her hands the moment they were wanted, with such a look of joy!!! Oh, happy, happy Mother in that hour and moment!"[10] To Eliza Sadler, she confided her satisfaction in seeing Annina "receive the last Sacraments with my sentiments of them".[11]

The afternoon before Rebecca's death, the little girl told her mother, "I have just been handing Our Lord my little cup. It is now quite full. He will come for me."[12] She referred, of course, to the cup of suffering that Jesus had asked James and John to drink; however, there is also a truly charming echo and consequence of what Elizabeth had told the child's dying father years before: "When you awake in *that* world, you will find that nothing could tempt you to return to *this.* You will see that your care over your wife and little ones was like a hand only, to hold the cup, which God Himself will give if He takes you."[13] That blessed cup of his daughter, held by him and handed over to God, was now full.

"At night the Superior came again, promising to stay with her to the last", Elizabeth continued in her *Journal.*

> At last, near four in the morning, she said: "Let me sit once more on the bed. It will be the last struggle." [Sister] Cecil beside her, Mother's arms lifting her, she sunk between us, but the darling head fell on its well-known heart it loved so well. After she seemed gone for awhile, nature made another push, and she said distinctly: "Ma, the girls talk so loud." "Think only of your dear Savior now, my darling," I said. "To be sure, certainly," she answered, and said no more, dropping her head for the last time on her Mother's heart.[14]

Father Dubois gave final witness to the scene: "The Mother is a miracle of divine favor. Night and day by the child, her health has not appeared to suffer. She held the child in her arms without dropping a tear, all the time of her agony and even eight minutes after she had died. *Mulierem fortem.*"[15] There can be no denying the remembrance of the *Pieta,* in soul and even physical imitation, of the mother with both her daughters.

The deathbeds of Mother Seton's spiritual daughters, each attended by her, brought her a like spiritual happiness. She put it into words in describing for Eliza Sadler the death of Sister Maria Murphy, who had brooked the disapproval of her own mother in joining the Lord's little band at Emmitsburg. The young Sister, overcome with joy at the approach of her Lord in Viaticum, had nearly fallen out of bed as she exclaimed, "O my Jesus, my dear Lord!" And Elizabeth rejoiced to Mrs. Sadler, "To have been, and to be still, *her Mother!* The natural one was *present,* but the *spiritual* one, who had all her dear little secrets of the soul, was the dearest."[16] Bruté rejoiced with her: "O happy Mother! Already three of your dear daughters in heaven, not counting the first two, the tender sisters whom your example has already led there. Give, give thanks, and redouble your zeal to follow these celestial souls."[17]

Death indeed came early and frequently to the young community, and the young in years were its special victims. The lines of tombstones with the inscribed ages—eighteen, nineteen, twenty— still stand in the "little sacred wood" as evidence of those sad and difficult first years.

Elizabeth and her Sisters faced the inevitable reality with faith and love. She trained them in heroic paths, and they followed readily and gladly. "*Death in desire* has many advantages", she told them. "1st, it is very agreeable to God, because by it we submit ourselves to Him as His creatures and offer ourselves a voluntary victim to His power and majesty. 2nd, it is very useful to ourselves, because it teaches us to die by degrees, it habituates us to the acts of virtue we would wish to make at Death, and to do beforehand what we would then desire to do." How quickly Mother Seton got down to hard tacks! The practical always caught her attention and preference:

3rd, those who are not in this practice are in danger of dying like animals, because the pain of the body so weighs down the mind that it can scarcely think of anything—but when we are versed in the art of dying, whatever the pains of the body may be, the soul will still be able to produce those acts which it has been long accustomed to form, or should it be so oppressed and stupefied as to be incapable of any exertion, what comfort then to have done repeatedly and in full consciousness, what its present condition makes so difficult, or perhaps impossible.[18]

Surely, Elizabeth's mind went back over the years to the death-beds of family and friends and the uneasiness they had brought her—Eliza Maitland's asking, "How is it, that until we are just going, we never think of the necessary dispositions to meet death?"[19]—friend Catherine Cooper, "Dying in the most melancholy manner, unconscious of the change she is making of this world for the next"[20]—and especially her "soul's sister", Rebecca Seton: "How many looks of silent distress have we exchanged about the last passage, this exchange of time for eternity!" she had confided to Amabilia Filicchi at the time. "To be sure, her uncommon piety and innocence and sweet confidence in God are my full consolation; but I mean to say that a departing soul has so many trials and temptations that, for my part, I go through a sort of agony never to be described—even while, to keep up their hope and courage, I appear to them most cheerful."[21] Elizabeth "could not . . . help the strong comparison of a sick and dying bed in your happy country, where the poor sufferer is soothed and strengthened at once by every help of religion; where the one you call *Father* of your soul attends and watches it in the weakness and trials of parting nature with the same care you and I watch our little infant's body in its first struggles and wants on its entrance into life."[22]

There was, of course, a desire for death that was wrong, Elizabeth warned her Sisters: "We often wish for death that we may be delivered from an unhappy life, and this desire is not good. We should never wish to get rid of our life because it is an unhappy one, or full of pains and trials; on the contrary, if there was no other evil in it, we should cherish and preserve it all in our power, since the more pains and trials we have in it, the greater sacrifices we may make to God, and the more we may prove our love to Him."[23]

That being said, "Consider that it is a great grace not to be afraid of death", Elizabeth assured them, "and it is a great perfection to desire it with a well-regulated desire according to God, for what virtue can the soul possess that is not contained in the desire of death? It possesses *humility,* since it is ready to receive all the humiliations of death, to return to dust and corruption. It possesses *poverty,* since it is ready to quit all that the world contains, and *chastity,* since it turns from all the world's joys and pleasures. Go over every virtue separately, you will find that the desire of death includes them all."[24]

Elizabeth could not fail to advance the most personal and intimate motive of all for vowed religious: "Consider death also as the coming of the heavenly Spouse, as is said in the parable of the virgins to whom He came by surprise at midnight—oh, how blessed His coming to those happy ones who were waiting for Him with a holy impatience."[25]

Elizabeth's own holy impatience is evident in the fervor and emphases of her writing. "Come, then, O Death!" she breaks forth at one point, "that I may no more offend my God, no more oppose *His Will*—come, take my soul, deliver it from this wretched frailty which makes it fall so often, and for what is in itself nothing—come, *I do desire* you, *desire you* with my whole heart."[26]

When Elizabeth's time of yearning was over, when her own turn came, she was gloriously ready. It was anticipated two years before the event with a sudden, downward rush of her powers. She was indeed ready, even straining forward. "Not even little acts for obtaining fear or anxiety about this death", she admitted blithely to Bruté, "can move that stronghold of peace, thanksgiving and abandon of every atom of life and its belongings to Him—even William I can see but in the great whole", she continued, surely with some amusement over past agonies for the cherished child and perhaps surprise at this newfound peace in God however proven before—"cannot cry, even for edification and duty"—

this is a spirit of mischief certainly. "You laugh. What [a] life indeed. A greyheaded carpenter whistling over the plank he measures for Ellen's coffin* —just beyond, the ground plowing to plant *potatoes,* just beyond again good *Jo* (I believe) making the pit to plant Ellen for her glorious resurrection—beautiful life, the whole delight *in God.* Oh, what relish in *that word!*"[27]

That ineffable word was the source of Elizabeth's happy contentment. "Nothing in our state of clouds and veils I can see so plainly as how the saints died of love and joy," she told Bruté, "since I so wretched and truly miserable can only read word after word of the blessed 83rd and 41st Psalms in unutterable feelings ever to our God through the thousand pressings and overflowings— God—God—God—that the supreme delight, that He is God, and to open the mouth and heart wide that He may fill it."[28]

Elizabeth's friends far and wide were alerted. Their response is positive testimony not only to her exceptional readiness but also to the proper face all God's sons and daughters should put upon what is, after all, His coming to welcome them to eternal bliss. As she put it simply to Bruté, "We talk now all day long of my death and how it will be just like the rest of the housework."[29] And that was a fair description of the way her friends took it, too, even her Protestant brother-in-law Dr. Wright Post, who wrote:

> Perhaps you have conceived your situation more critical than it really is. . . . It may yet please God to restore you to that useful- ness which has always marked the sphere in which you moved. That this may be His Will is my most fervent prayer. But should it be otherwise, should He in His wise and righteous Providence deem it proper to remove you from this world of care and disquietude, what shall I say, my dear Sister? Nothing. Nothing is necessary to a mind already familiarized to the prospect of a change which sooner or later must be realized, and which is so well disciplined in the way which leads to that place of blessed- ness where the anxieties of this life cease from troubling, and the weary are at rest.[30]

---

* Sister Ellen Brady.

He quite rightly, too, refused to keep the news of Elizabeth's decline from her sister, his wife.

Father Babade wrote in a very matter-of-fact way, foreign to his reputation for sighs and tears: "Ten years are passed; your work is consolidated. I desire nothing more for you but a happy death. . . . I would like very much to see you before you die, but I foresee that the Superior will not allow me to go to Emmitsburg in the present state of things. . . . As soon as I hear of your death I will say Mass for the repose of your dear soul. . . . If you find mercy, as I hope you will, do not forget above this one who has thought so much of you here below."[31] Bishop Cheverus wrote as simply, but his own sanctity is in the few words: "I do not pity you. I envy your situation, running now to the embrace of Him who is love. . . . You are most frequently remembered at the altar and will be so long as I shall celebrate the Holy Mysteries. Pray for me here and in heaven."[32]

Elizabeth herself told Antonio Filicchi the news in her most casual vein but with the mixture of intimate banter and serious spiritual friendship that characterizes all her letters to him. "It is rather suspected that I, your poor little sister, am about to go and meet your Filippo,"[*] she began, "but nothing of health can be certain and calculated at my age, 45. I may recover and crack nuts yet with my nose and chin, as they say; *I know not.* All I know is, we must all be ready for this dear, dearest thief who is to come when least expected. I go almost every day to communion (as my good confessor and superior says, thro' *condescension to my weakness*)"—she could never resist the native mischievousness raised in her by the solemn Father Dubois—"so if you good people are not *very* good over the water, it is no fault of my prayers; and I hope I shall not be forgotten in yours, to *which* I so well owe all that I possess: *my blessed Faith.* "[33]

The quiet ecstasy of Elizabeth's soul was reserved, of course, for her director. "Mind not my health", she chaffed Gabriel Bruté.

[*] Filippo Filicchi had died in 1816.

Death grins broader in the pot every morning [when she saw her reflection as she washed], and I grin at him and I show him his master. Oh, be blessed, blessed, blessed. I see nothing in this world but blue skies and our altars. All the rest is so plainly not to be looked at, but all left to Him, with tears only for sin. We talk now all day long of my death and how it will be just like the rest of the housework. What is it else? What came in the world for? Why in it so long? But this last great eternal end—it seems to me so simple, when I look up at the crucifix simpler still; so that I went to sleep before I made any thanksgiving but *Te Deum* and *Magnificat* after communion. . . .

This morning, Our *Adored Harp* pressed close on the aching breast, we swept every sacred chord of praise and thanksgiving. Then, weeping under the willows of that horrid Babylon whose waters are drunk so greedily while our heavenly streams pass by unheeded, the silent heart is pressed closer and closer. G[abriel] Blessed, mind not my follies. I see the everlasting hills so near and the door of my eternity so wide open that I turn too wild sometimes.[34]

Elizabeth's same wondrous understanding of death, the same mystical longing, lasted the two years remaining God ordained for her. Acknowledging the arrival of Father John Hickey's most recent letter, five months before the end, Elizabeth wrote:

Poor, dying, good Sister Jane was present and I let her share the kiss of peace, which she did with starting tears, feeling so well her condition to be hopeless in the senseless language of this world. Oh, my father, friend, could I hear my last stage of cough and feel my last stage of pain and the tearing away of my prison walls, how would I bear my joy? "*The thought of going home, called out by His Will*—what a transport! But they say: 'Don't you fear to die?' Such a sinner must fear, but I fear much more to live and know what I do: that every evening examen finds my account but lengthened and enlarged. I don't fear death half so much as my hateful, vile self."[35]

In one of the long night watches Elizabeth talked with Sister Cecilia O'Conway, her nurse, of "departed friends, present suffering compared to the ... suffering of Purgatory, of souls dying in misery without the sacraments". Suddenly she began to cry. "I am ashamed to complain when I remember those dear ones who have gone", she sobbed. "What agonies they must have suffered—! Their poor, bleeding bones—! That sweet, lovely Rebecca that I told you of, though not a Catholic, who suffered such bitter pain with such happy disposition!"

Kissing Elizabeth's hand, Cecilia said soothingly, "O my soul's Mother, Our Lord who knows your desires perhaps will realize your wish of suffering a long time on this bed of sickness. May He grant you your Purgatory in this life, and in death may you fly to His bosom of peace and rest."

"My blessed God," protested the dying Mother, raising her eyes to heaven, "how far from that thought am I, of going straight to heaven—such a miserable creature as I am!"[36] It was a protest from the depths of her heart, for, Bruté has witnessed, "a soul who felt so sacredly, with such light, the holiness of her God, had no doubt of Purgatory, had no presumption that it would not be for her".[37]

It was surely fitting for this humble, loving soul to receive, even on this side of the grave, what very few others receive, a clean bill of spiritual health. "My good Mother, your poor physician of the soul does not see you much, as he does not wish to fatigue you", read the note that Bruté handed Elizabeth.

He has no cause to fear, knowing that the heavenly Physician, the Beloved, the Spouse, the Only Desire of your heart, is continually present: present in the love, confidence, abandon, which He inspires, abandon the most tender and most unreserved—present in the continual acts of penance, humility, dependence and resignation to suffer everything in union with Him, with His cross—present in the peace, the tranquil joy which He imparts; in the total disengagement which He teaches; in the grace of every moment, pain or comfort which He dispenses.[38]

After Elizabeth's death Bruté's apostolic spirit struggled to express what would forever remain inexpressible, "Her magnanimous faith on her deathbed! My Lord, I have seen it, felt it. Express it I cannot, and I suffer immensely in not being able to do so, for it would be a source of so much edification if it could be communicated such as I FELT IT."[39]

NOTES

Chapter One
"She Is a Saint"

[1] In a conversation with the writer.

[2] On a television panel with the writer.

[3] Mary Carson, "Let's Speed up Canonization".

[4] A. Tanqueray. *Synopsis Theologiae Dogmaticae Fundamentalis,* vol. I (Paris, Tournai and Rome, 1935), no. 931.

[5] Paul VI, Canonization of St. Elizabeth Ann Seton, St. Peter's Square, Sept. 14, 1975.

[6] Paul VI, *Homily.*

[7] Charles I. White, *Life of Mrs. Eliza A. Seton,* p. 362.

[8] Joseph Bernardin, *Statement on Canonization of St. Elizabeth Ann Seton.*

[9] John Cardinal Wright, *Address.*

[10] Cf. Rom 8:29. Paul VI, op. cit.

[11] Paul VI, op. cit.

[12] Archives of St. Joseph's Provincial House (hereafter referred to as "ASJPH"), X, 10, Seton to Filicchi, Winter 1805–6.

[13] Ibid.

[14] ASJPH, X, 3a, Seton to Filicchi, Mar. 14, 1805.

[15] Archives of Georgetown University, Washington, D.C. (hereafter referred to as "AGU"), 240:7, Seton to Hickey, June 10, 1819.

[16] ASJPH, XII, 15, July 5, 1821.

[17] Ibid., May 19, 1821.

Chapter Two
"... And Then Eternity"

[1] ASJPH, *Dear Remembrances.*
[2] Ibid.

[3] Ibid.

[4] Ibid.

[5] Heb 13:14.

[6] ASJPH, *Dear Remembrances.*

[7] Ibid.

[8] Ibid.

[9] Ibid.

[10] Ibid.

[11] Archives of the Sisters of Charity of Halifax, Nova Scotia (hereafter referred to as "ASCH"), S–J Coll., Seton to Seton, Feb. 19, 1811.

[12] ASJPH, *Dear Remembrances.*

[13] Ibid.

[14] Ibid.

[15] Francis Thompson, *The Hound of Heaven.*

[16] ASJPH, VI, 81, Seton to Scott, Mar. 26, 1810.

[17] Ibid.

[18] Ibid., 16, Seton to Scott, Fall 1798.

[19] Ibid., VIII, 30, Seton to Sadler, 1801.

[20] Ibid., VI, 47, Seton to Scott, Fall 1802.

[21] Ibid., XVII, 14.

[22] Ibid., XII, 102, Seton to Weis, 1812.

[23] Ibid., VII, 47, Seton to Sadler, May 1812.

[24] Ibid., VI, 96, Seton to Scott, Jan. 25, 1813.

[25] *Strong woman:* the reference is to Prov 31:10–31. The passage was read in St. Elizabeth Ann's canonization mass and is assigned by the Church to one of her approved masses; ASJPH, XII, 81, Dubois to Bruté, Nov. 1816.

[26] Ibid., XII, B14, Aug. 20, 1818.

[27] ASJPH, IX, 2, Seton to Seton, Nov. 25, 1814.

[28] Ibid., S–J Coll., Seton to Seton, 1818.

[29] Archives of the Sisters of Charity of St. Elizabeth, Convent, N.J. (hereafter referred to as "ASCSE"), S–J Coll., Seton to Seton, Apr. 5, 1818.

[30] ASCSE, S–J Coll., 97, Seton to Filicchi, Dec. 1815.

[31] Ibid., 128, Seton to Filicchi, Oct. 1820.

[32] Ibid., IX, 6, Seton to Seton, Summer 1815.

[33] Ibid., S–J Coll., Seton to Seton, Feb. 14, 1817.

[34] Archives of Notre Dame University, Notre Dame, Ind. (hereafter

referred to as "ANDU"), Seton to Seton, July 23, 1820.
[35] Archives of the Sisters of Charity of St. Vincent de Paul, Mount St. Vincent-on-Hudson, N.Y. (hereafter referred to as AMSV), Seton to Seton, Mar. 24, 1818.
[36] ASJPH, XII, B14, Aug. 20, 1818.
[37] Ibid., 3.

Chapter Three
"His Blessed Will"

[1] ASJPH, VI, 53, Seton to Scott, July 1804.
[2] Ibid., 81, Seton to Scott, Mar. 26, 1810.
[3] Acts 26:14.
[4] ASJPH, XII, 78, Seton to Bruté, Nov. 1818.
[5] Ibid., III, 6.
[6] Ibid., XII, 12, May 19, 1821.
[7] Ibid.
[8] Ibid., 100.
[9] Ibid., *Dear Remembrances.*
[10] Ibid.
[11] Ibid.
[12] Ibid., III, 6.
[13] Ibid.
[14] Ibid., 8.
[15] Ibid.
[16] William Seton died at Pisa, Italy, on Dec. 27, 1803, scarcely a week after his release from a month's confinement in the *lazaretto;* Elizabeth Seton was received into the Catholic Church by Father Matthew O'Brien in St. Peter's, New York City, on Mar. 14, 1805.
[17] ASJPH, VIII, 145.
[18] Ibid., S–F Coll., 29, Seton to Filicchi, Fall 1807.
[19] Eight State Street, on the Battery, had been Elizabeth Seton's last home with her husband and children, 1801–3. It is now her shrine church in New York City; the Quarantine was the health station of Elizabeth's father, Dr. Richard Bayley, on Staten Island, where she and her family spent happy summers with him and where he died in her arms, Aug. 17, 1801; ASJPH, VII, 35, Seton to Sadler, June 9, 1808.

[20] Ibid., VIII, 154.
[21] Ibid., S–F Coll., 76, Seton to Filicchi, Aug. 20, 1808.
[22] Ibid., 50, Seton to Filicchi, Oct. 11, 1805.
[23] Ibid., 26, Seton to Filicchi, Aug. 1806.
[24] Ibid., 76, Seton to Filicchi, Aug. 20, 1808.
[25] Ibid., 30, Seton to Filicchi, July 8, 1808.
[26] Ibid., VIII, 153, Seton to Seton, Oct. 6, 1808.
[27] Ibid., 152, Seton to Seton, Aug. 1808.
[28] Ibid., VI, 77, Seton to Scott, Summer 1808.
[29] Ibid., 74, Seton to Scott, Dec. 1808.
[30] Ibid., S–F Coll., 34, Seton to Filicchi, Feb. 8, 1809.
[31] Ibid., 76, Seton to Filicchi, Aug. 20, 1808.
[32] Ibid., 34, Seton to Filicchi, Feb. 8, 1809.
[33] Ibid., 109, Seton to Filicchi, Summer 1817.
[34] ASJPH, S–F Coll., 34, Seton to Filicchi, Feb. 8, 1809.
[35] Ibid., *Annales,* 1882, II, 71, Dubourg to Elévès, July 15, 1818.
[36] Ibid., VI, 77, Seton to Scott, Mar. 23, 1809.
[37] White, op. cit., p. 252.
[38] ASJPH, III, 18.
[39] Ibid., 26, O'Conway to Seton, Summer 1813.
[40] Ibid., XII, 17b.
[41] Ibid.
[42] Ibid., 40, Seton to Bruté, n.d.
[43] St. Vincent de Paul, *Correspondance, Entretins, Documents,* XI, p. 119.
[44] ASJPH, XII, 16, Bruté to Seton, Aug. 1820.
[45] Ibid., 76, Seton to Bruté, c. 1820.
[46] Ibid., 13.
[47] Archives of the Archdiocese of Baltimore, Baltimore, Md. (hereafter referred to as "AB"), 7-M-7, Seton to Carroll, Nov. 14, 1809.
[48] ASJPH, XIX, 5, Seton to O'Conway, July 1810.
[49] White, op. cit., p. 425.
[50] ASJPH, I, 42, Carroll to Seton, Mar. 1800.
[51] Ibid., 43, Carroll to Seton, Mar. 1811.
[52] Ibid., VIII, 154, Seton to Seton, Apr. 3, 1809.
[53] AB, 7-M-6, Seton to Carroll, Nov. 2, 1809.
[54] ASJPH, XII, 102, Seton to Weis, Aug. 9, 1810.
[55] Ibid., II, 60, Seton to Weis, Summer 1811.

[56] AB, 7-N-13, Seton to Carroll, Sept. 5, 1811.

[57] ASJPH, I, 45, Carroll to Seton, Sept. 1811.

[58] Ibid.

[59] Ibid.

[60] Ibid.

[61] Ibid., VIII, 49, Seton to Sadler, Spring 1812.

[62] Ibid., VI, 80, Seton to Scott, Jan. 1810.

[63] Ibid., XII, 346, Seton to Bruté, Fall 1812.

[64] AGU, 240:7, Seton to Hickey, June 10, 1819.

[65] ASJPH, XII, 2.

[66] White, op. cit., p. 340.

[67] ASJPH, VIII, 145; cf. also VII, 13, 18, 19, Seton letters to Sadler, Summer 1799.

[68] Ibid., VI, 79, Seton to Scott, Sept. 20, 1809.

[69] Mary Bayley Post was Elizabeth Seton's sister; ASJPH, S–F Coll., 97, Seton to Filicchi, Nov. 1815.

Chapter Four
"Prayer of the Heart"

[1] ASJPH, III, 11.

[2] Ibid., 6.

[3] Ibid.

[4] Ibid., *Notebook, Meditations and Instructions.*

[5] Ibid.

[6] Ibid.

[7] Ibid., XII, 32, Seton to Bruté, n.d.

[8] Ibid., *Notebook, Meditations and Instructions.*

[9] Ibid.

[10] Ibid.

[11] Ibid.

[12] Ibid.

[13] Ibid., XII, 44, Seton to Bruté, n.d.

[14] Ibid., *Notebook, Meditations and Instructions.*

[15] Ibid.

[16] Ibid., III, 81.

[17] Ibid., XVII, 14.

18 Ibid.

19 Ibid.

20 Ibid.

21 White, op. cit., p. 106.

22 ASJPH, VIII, 153, Seton to Seton, Oct. 3, 1808.

23 Ibid., S–F Coll., Seton to Filicchi, Aug. 20, 1808.

24 Ibid., *Annales,* 1882, 34, Dubourg to Elévè, July 15, 1828.

25 Ibid.

26 Ibid., VII, 43, Seton to Sadler, Aug. 3, 1810.

27 Joseph I. Dirvin, C.M., *Mrs. Seton,* pp. 250–51.

28 ASJPH, XVII, 14, Seton to Seton, Nov. 19, 1803.

29 Ibid., Nov. 24, 1803.

30 Ibid., S–F Coll., Seton to Filicchi, Aug. 30, 1804.

31 Ibid., XII, 69, Seton to Bruté, [1816].

32 Ibid., I, 38, Carroll to Filicchi, Fall 1804.

33 White, op. cit., p. 344.

34 ASJPH, XII, 50, Seton to Bruté, Dec. 1815.

35 Ibid., III, 21.

36 Ibid., XII, 99, Seton to Weis, May 13, 1810, postscript, copy in Bruté's hand, Jan. 4, 1822.

37 Ibid., III, 26, Seton to Bruté, June 13, 1815.

38 Ibid., IX, 3, Seton to Seton, Mar. 1815.

39 Ibid., X, 14, Filicchi to Seton, Fall 1804.

40 Ibid., 33, Filicchi to Seton, Sept. 1805.

41 Ibid., I, 121, Matignon to Seton, Sept. 1805.

42 Ibid., III, 26, Seton to Bruté, Spring 1815.

43 Ibid., *Notebook, Meditations and Instructions.*

44 Ibid., uncatalogued, Seton to Seton, Oct. 7, 1805.

Chapter Five
"Our Lord and Our Lady"

1 ASJPH, X, 3a, Seton to Filicchi, Jan. 1805.

2 Cf. John A. Hardon, *The Protestant Churches in America* (Westminster, 1956), p. 39.

3 ASJPH, III, 8.

4 Dirvin, op. cit., p. 106.

[5] ASJPH, VIII, 60, Seton to Seton, Spring 1804.

[6] Ibid., *Dear Remembrances.*

[7] Ibid., III, 15, *Leghorn Journal.*

[8] Ibid.

[9] Ibid.

[10] Ibid.

[11] Ibid., VIII, 60, Seton to Seton, Spring 1804.

[12] ASJPH, VIII, 60, Spring 1804.

[13] Ibid., *Dear Remembrances.*

[14] Ibid.

[15] Ibid.

[16] Ibid.; White, op. cit., p. 106.

[17] ASJPH, VIII, 60, Seton to Seton, Apr. 1804.

[18] Ibid., S–F Coll., 4, Seton to Filicchi, Aug. 30, 1804.

[19] Ibid., X, 3a, Seton to Filicchi, Aug.–Sept. 1804.

[20] Ibid.

[21] Ibid., X, 3a, Seton to Filicchi, Feb. 27, 1805.

[22] Ibid., Mar. 25, 1805.

[23] Ibid.

[24] Ibid.

[25] Ibid.

[26] Ibid., S–F Coll., Seton to Filicchi, Spring 1805.

[27] Ibid., *Dear Remembrances.*

[28] *Pange Lingua Gloriosa,* eucharistic hymn by St. Thomas Aquinas.

[29] ASJPH, X, 3a, Seton to Filicchi, Spring 1805.

[30] Ibid.

[31] Ibid., S–F Coll., 29, Seton to Filicchi, Spring 1805.

[32] Ibid., VIII, 145.

[33] Ibid.

[34] Ibid.

[35] Ibid., 154, Seton to Seton, June 15, 1808.

[36] Ibid., Easter 1809.

[37] Ibid., XII, 38.

[38] Ibid., 47, Seton to Bruté, n.d.

[39] Ibid., 57.

[40] Ibid., *Notebook, Meditations and Instructions.*

[41] Ibid., III, 43.

[42] Ibid., XII, 78.

[43] Ibid., VIII, 145.

[44] Ibid., 38.

[45] Ibid., XI, 25.

[46] Ibid., XII, 2.

[47] Ibid., 38.

[48] Ibid., 14 — "O woman, great is your faith."

[49] Ibid., VIII, 60, Seton to Seton, Winter–Spring 1804.

[50] Ibid.

[51] St. Bernard of Clairvaux, "Sermo in dom. infra oct. Assumptionis", 14–15: *Opera Omnia,* Edit. Cisterc. 5 (1968), 273–74.

[52] ASJPH, X, 3, Seton to Filicchi, Summer 1804.

[53] Ibid., 9, Seton to Filicchi, Fall 1804.

[54] Ibid.

[55] Ibid., 30, Seton to Filicchi, Jan. 1805.

[56] Ibid., III, 18.

[57] Ibid., XII, 33, Sept. 1812.

[58] Ibid., *Dear Remembrances,* Aug. 15, 1813.

[59] Ibid.

[60] Ibid., III, 42.

[61] Ibid., XII, 36, Seton to Bruté, n.d.

[62] Ibid., III, 42.

[63] Ibid., XI, 28, Seton to Post, c. 1816.

[64] Ibid., XII, 6.

[65] Ibid., 5.

Chapter Six
"If You Would Be My Disciple . . . "

[1] Lk 9:23.

[2] ASJPH, *Spiritual Journal.*

[3] Ibid., Apr. 18, 1800.

[4] Ibid., *Dear Remembrances.*

[5] Ibid., III, 7, Sunday, first day of Aug. 1802, five o'clock in the afternoon.

[6] Ibid., *Notebook, Meditations and Instructions.*

[7] Ibid.

[8] Ibid., VIII, 88, Seton to Seton, Oct. 2, 1803.

[9] Ibid., XVIII, 14, Nov. 23, 1803.

[10] Ibid., Dec. 14, 1803.

[11] Ibid., X, 3.

[12] Ibid., VI, 53, Seton to Scott, July 1804.

[13] Ibid., 44, Seton to Scott, Fall 1801.

[14] Ibid., VIII, 37.

[15] Ibid., VIII, 60, Seton to Seton, Spring 1804.

[16] Ibid., III, 14c.

[17] White, op. cit., p. 110.

[18] ASJPH, S–F Coll., 107, Seton to Filicchi, Apr. 4, 1817.

[19] Ibid., X, 3a, Seton to Filicchi, Mar. 20, 1805.

[20] Ibid., Seton to Filicchi, Jan. 1805.

[21] Ibid., Seton to Filicchi, Mar. 20, 1805.

[22] Ibid., Seton to Filicchi, Spring 1805.

[23] ASCSE, S–J Coll., Seton to Seton, July 25, 1817.

[24] ASJPH, III, 18.

[25] Ibid., S–F Coll., 53, Seton to Filicchi, Summer 1805.

[26] Ibid.

[27] Ibid.

[28] Ibid., XI, 1, Sadler to Seton, Fall 1805.

[29] Ibid., VI, 60, Seton to Scott, Fall 1805.

[30] Ibid., 61, Seton to Scott, Jan. 20, 1806.

[31] Ibid.

[32] Ibid., I, 22, Tisserant to Seton, Mar. 9, 1806.

[33] AB, 7-M-7, Seton to Carroll, Jan. 25, 1810.

[34] ASJPH, I, 44, Carroll to Seton, July 1810.

[35] Ibid., VII, 43, Seton to Sadler, Aug. 3, 1810.

[36] Ibid., *Minutes,* Aug. 20, 1814.

[37] Ibid., *Mother Rose's Journal,* 26–27; ibid., XII, 102, Seton to Weis, Aug. 9, 1810.

[38] Ibid., XII, 102, Seton to Weis, Aug. 9, 1810.

[39] Ibid., 99, Seton to Weis, May 13, 1810, copy in Bruté's hand, Jan. 4, 1822.

[40] Ibid., Mar. 19, 1814.

[41] Ibid.

[42] Ibid.

[43] Ibid., Aug. 26, 1813.

[44] Ibid., 1813.

[45] Ibid., Aug. 9, 1809 or 1810.

[46] Ibid., July 30, 1812.

[47] Ibid., Aug. 28, 1810.

[48] Ibid., n.d.

[49] Ibid., n.d.

[50] Ibid.

[51] Ibid., 102, Seton to Weis, Mar. 26, 1813.

[52] Ibid., *Notebook, Meditations and Instructions.*

[53] Ibid., III, 18.

[54] Ibid., XII, 108, Bruté to Filicchi, May 5, 1821.

[55] AMSV, Seton to Boyle, Oct. 8, 1820.

[56] White, op. cit., p. 340.

[57] Ibid.

[58] Ibid.

[59] Ibid., p. 344.

[60] Ibid.

[61] Ibid., p. 342.

[62] Ibid., p. 417.

[63] Ibid., p. 425.

[64] Ibid., p. 418.

[65] Ibid.

[66] ASJPH, XII, 70, Seton to Bruté, Oct. 1814.

[67] Ibid., III, 26, Seton to Bruté, June 1815.

[68] White, op. cit., pp. 416–17.

[69] Prayer of Pope Pius VII. Cf. Dirvin, op. cit., p. 454.

Chapter Seven
"A Kind of John the Baptist"

[1] Dirvin, op. cit., p. 390.

[2] ASJPH, XII, 55, Seton to Bruté, Sept. 2, 1816.

[3] Archives of the Sisters of Charity of Cincinnati, Ohio (hereafter referred to as "ASCC"), S–J Coll., Seton to Seton, July 27, 1794.

[4] ASCSE, S–J Coll., Seton to Seton, June 10, 1801.

[5] ASJPH, VIII, 60, Seton to Seton, Apr. 1804.

[6] Ibid., *Dear Remembrances.*

[7] Ibid., VIII, 18, Seton to Seton, c. 1801.

[8] Ibid., 32, Seton to Seton, Aug. 1802.

[9] Ibid., 28, Seton to Seton, Summer 1803.

[10] Robert Nelson, Protestant spiritual writer.
[11] ASJPH, VIII, 28, Summer 1803; ibid., 5.
[12] Ibid., 54.
[13] Ibid., XVII, 14, Nov. 30, 1803.
[14] Ibid., Dec. 12, 1803.
[15] Ibid., Dec. 13, 1803.
[16] Ibid., III, 8, Seton to Seton, Dec. 1803.
[17] Ibid., VIII, 60, Seton to Seton, Dec. 1803.
[18] Ibid., X, 3, Seton to Filicchi, Summer 1804.
[19] Ibid., VI, 83, Seton to Scott, July 20, 1810.
[20] Ibid., VII, 65, Seton to Dupleix, Feb. 11, 1811.
[21] AB, 7-N-11, Seton to Carroll, May 13, 1811.
[22] Cf. Dirvin, op. cit., p. 158.
[23] ASJPH, IX, 28, Seton to Seton, 1806.
[24] Ibid., VI, 83, Seton to Scott, July 18, 1810.
[25] Ibid., IX, 49a, Seton to Seton, June 28, 1813.
[26] Ibid., Seton to Seton, Apr. 1814.
[27] Ibid., VI, 95, Seton to Scott, Sept. 1812.
[28] Ibid.
[29] Ibid., IX, 43, Seton to Seton, Sept. 1815.
[30] Ibid., 46, Seton to Seton, 1815.
[31] Ibid., XII, 62, Seton to Bruté, June 29, 1816.
[32] Ibid., XII, 18, Seton to Seton, Mar. 1815.
[33] AMSV, S–J Coll., Seton to Seton, 1816.
[34] Archives of the Daughters of Charity, Western Province, St. Louis, Mo. (hereafter referred to as "ADCWP"), S–J Coll., Seton to Seton, May 8, 1820.
[35] ASJPH, XII, 8, Seton to Wiseman, June 29, 1820.
[36] AGU, 240:7, Seton to Hickey, July 2, 1820.
[37] ASJPH, S–F Coll., 97, Nov. 1815.
[38] Ibid., *Dear Remembrances.*
[39] Ibid., XV, 12, Seton to Seton, Spring 1801.
[40] Ibid., X, 3a, Seton to Filicchi, June–July 1804.
[41] Cf. Dirvin, op. cit., pp. 180–81 and passim.
[42] ASJPH, IV, 168, Seton to Ogden, June 17, 1806.
[43] AMSV, *Red Diary.*
[44] ASJPH, I, 121, Matignon to Seton, Aug. 1806.
[45] Ibid., 34, Matignon to Seton, 1806.
[46] Ibid., S–F Coll., 50, Seton to Filicchi, Oct. 11, 1805.

47 Ibid., 26, Seton to Filicchi, Aug. 1806.

48 Ibid., VI, 71, Seton to Scott, Apr. 1808.

49 Ibid., 77, Seton to Scott, 1808.

50 Ibid., VIII, 153, Seton to Seton, Oct. 3, 1808.

51 Ibid., I, 10, Cheverus to Seton, Apr. 13, 1809.

52 Ibid., VI, 77, Seton to Scott, Mar. 23, 1809.

53 Ibid., *Dear Remembrances.*

54 Ibid.

55 Ibid.

56 Cf. Dirvin, op. cit., pp. 55ff.

57 Cf. ibid., pp. 54, 56 and passim.

58 ASJPH, VII, 5, Seton to Sadler, Mar. 1798.

59 Ibid., VI, 43, Seton to Scott, Fall 1801.

60 Ibid., VII, 7, Seton to Sadler, June 1798.

61 Ibid., VI, 12, Seton to Scott, Oct. 1798.

62 Ibid., 45, Feb. 1802.

63 Ibid., VIII, 37.

64 Ibid., *Dear Remembrances.*

65 Ibid.

66 Ibid., *Sisters of Charity Meditate the Means of Making Well Their Retreat.*

67 Ibid., *Retreat Meditations,* July 1813.

68 Ibid.

69 Ibid.

70 Ibid., XII, 13, Simon Gabriel Bruté, *Notes,* May 19, 1821.

71 Ibid., *Annales,* 1882, II, 71, Dubourg to Elévès, July 15, 1828.

72 Cf. Dirvin, op. cit., p. 303.

73 ASJPH, VI, 77, Seton to Scott, Mar. 23, 1809.

74 Dirvin, op. cit., pp. 276–77, 324.

75 ASJPH, VI, 84, Seton to Scott, Fall 1810.

76 AB, Seton to Harper, Jan. 2, 1812.

77 Dirvin, op. cit., pp. 397–98.

78 ASJPH, S–F Coll., 114, Seton to Filicchi, Aug. 1818.

79 Ibid., XII, B6, Seton to Wiseman, Nov. 27, 1815.

80 Ibid., III, 26, *Journal* for Bruté, 1815.

81 Ibid., XII, 6, O'Conway to Bruté, Jan. 1821.

82 Paul VI, *Remarks.*

83 ASJPH, *Dear Remembrances.*

84 AMSV, S–J Coll., Seton to Bayley, n.d. [1798].

85 Ibid., VI, 34, Seton to Scott, Jan. 1801.

86 Ibid.

87 Ibid., VIII, 87.

88 Ibid., VI, 71, Seton to Scott, Apr. 1808.

89 Ibid., VIII, 154, Seton to Seton, June 1808.

90 AMSV, Dubourg to Seton, May 27, 1808.

91 ASJPH, S–F Coll., 32, Seton to Filicchi, Jan. 16, 1809.

92 Ibid., 34, Seton to Filicchi, Feb. 8, 1809.

93 White, op. cit., p. 275.

94 AMSV, I, 23, Dubourg to Seton, Dec. 28, 1809.

95 ASJPH, S–F Coll., 109, Seton to Filicchi, Summer 1817.

96 Ibid., 114, Seton to Filicchi, Aug. 1818.

97 Paul VI, *Remarks.*

98 Ibid.

99 Dirvin, op. cit., p. 325.

100 ASJPH, III, 48b.

101 White, op. cit., p. 362.

102 Ibid., pp. 363–64.

103 Ibid., p. 364.

104 Ibid., p. 348.

105 ASJPH, III, 11, Seton to Caufmann, n.d.

106 Ibid., XII, 5, Seton to Wiseman, Oct. 14, 1815.

107 Ibid., 15, Seton to Wiseman, Summer 1818.

108 Ibid., 8, Seton to Wiseman, Aug. 12, 1813.

109 Ibid., B 9, Seton to anon., Apr. 6, 1813.

110 Ibid.

111 Ibid., IV, 100, Bonaparte to Seton, n.d.

112 Ibid.

113 Ibid., *Notebook, Meditations and Instructions,* Feb. 2, 1813.

114 ANDU, Egan to Seton, Jan. 6, 1826.

115 Ibid., XII, 108, Bruté to Filicchi, May 5, 1821.

116 Ibid., VII, 81, Seton to Smith, n.d. [1817].

117 Ibid., VIII, 2, Seton to Seton, 1801.

118 Ibid., XII, Seton to Bruté, n.d.

119 Ibid.

120 Ibid., 73, Seton to Bruté, Aug. 1, 1817.

121 Archives of Mount St. Mary's College, Emmitsburg, Md. (hereafter referred to as "AMSM"), Gellespie to Hickey, July 21, 1817.

122 ANDU, Egan to Seton, June 19, 1822.

[123] See above, p. 77.

[124] White, op. cit., p. 434.

[125] Dirvin, op. cit., pp. 431–32.

[126] Ibid., p. 432.

[127] James Roosevelt Bayley, *Memoirs of the Rt. Rev. Simon Wm. Gabriel Bruté, D.D.,* p. 40.

[128] ASJPH, III, 26, Seton to Bruté, Dec. 1814.

[129] Ibid., Seton to Bruté, *Journal* written for him by Mother Seton at his own request.

[130] Ibid.

[131] Ibid., XII, 50, Seton to Bruté, Dec. 1815.

[132] Ibid., 56.

[133] Ibid.

[134] Ibid., 41.

[135] Ibid., 76.

[136] AGU, 240:7, Seton to Hickey, July 2, 1820.

[137] Ibid., n.d.

[138] ASJPH, XII, 66, Seton to Bruté, Aug. 1818.

Chapter Eight
"My Blessed Faith"

[1] Vatican Council II, *Dogmatic Constitution on the Church (Lumen Gentium),* I, 8.

[2] Ibid.

[3] Ibid.

[4] Paul VI, *Homily.*

[5] Ibid.

[6] ASJPH, III, 29.

[7] Ibid., X, 3, Seton to Filicchi, July 1804.

[8] Ibid., XII, 80, Seton to Bruté, Summer 1816.

[9] Ibid., XI, b19, Sadler to Bruté, 1816.

[10] Ibid., XII, 80, Seton to Bruté, Summer 1816.

[11] Ibid.

[12] Ibid.

[13] Dirvin, op. cit., p. 129.

[14] ASJPH, X, 1, Filicchi to Seton, Jan. 9, 1804.

[15] Ibid., VIII, 60, *Journal* for Rebecca Seton.

[16] Ibid.

[17] Cf. Dirvin, op. cit., chap. XI.

[18] ASJPH, X, 3, Seton to Filicchi, July 1804.

[19] Ibid., S–F Coll., 6, Seton to Filicchi, Sept. 1804.

[20] Ibid., 4, Seton to Filicchi, Aug. 30, 1804.

[21] Phil 2:6.

[22] 2 Cor 8:9; Lk 4:18.

[23] Vatican Council II, *Dogmatic Constitution on the Church* (*Lumen Gentium*), I, 8.

[24] ASJPH, I, 38, Carroll to Filicchi, 1804.

[25] Ibid., X, 9, Seton to Filicchi, 1804.

[26] Ibid., 14, Filicchi to Seton, 1804.

[27] Ibid., X, 9, Seton to Filicchi, 1804.

[28] Ibid., S–F Coll., 6, Seton to Filicchi, 1804.

[29] Ibid., X, 3a, Seton to Filicchi, Jan. 1805.

[30] Ibid., XII, 80, Seton to Bruté, Summer 1816.

[31] AMSV, Cheverus to Seton, Mar. 4, 1805.

[32] ASJPH, X, 3a, Seton to Filicchi, Mar. 14, 1805.

[33] Vatican Council II, *Dogmatic Constitution on the Church* (*Lumen Gentium*), I, 8.

[34] ASJPH, XII, 68, Seton to Bruté, Dec. 26, 1816.

[35] Ibid., S–F Coll., 29, Seton to Filicchi, May 1805.

[36] White, op. cit., p. 340.

[37] ASJPH, II, 95, Seton to Filicchi, Spring 1805.

[38] Ibid., X, 3a, Seton to Filicchi, Mar. 1805.

[39] Ibid., S–F Coll., 29, Seton to Filicchi, Apr.–May 1805.

[40] Ibid., X, 3a, Seton to Filicchi, Jan. 1805.

[41] Ibid., Seton to Filicchi, Mar. 14, 1805.

[42] Ibid., Seton to Filicchi, Mar. 20, 1805.

[43] Ibid., S–F Coll., 64, Seton to Filicchi, May 1806.

[44] Ibid., XII, 1.

[45] Vatican Council II, *Dogmatic Constitution on the Church* (*Lumen Gentium*), I, 8.

[46] Ibid., 7.

[47] Cf. ibid., 8.

[48] Ibid., II, 10.

[49] St. Thérèse of Lisieux, *The Story of a Soul,* Chap. IX, quoted in the Second Reading, Office of Readings, Oct. 1, *The Liturgy of the Hours,* vol. 4 (New York, 1975).

[50] St. Augustine, *Sermo 25,* 7–8, PL 46, 937–38, quoted in the Second Reading, Office of Readings, Presentation of Mary, Nov. 21, *The Liturgy of the Hours,* vol. 4 (New York, 1975).

[51] ASJPH, XII, 7.

[52] AB, 7-M-6, Seton to Carroll, Nov. 2, 1809.

[53] ASJPH, XII, 3.

[54] Ibid., 13.

[55] Ibid., S–F Coll., 76, Seton to Filicchi, Aug. 20, 1808.

[56] Ibid., 34, Seton to Filicchi, Feb. 8, 1809.

[57] AB, 7-N-13, Seton to Carroll, Sept. 5, 1811.

[58] Ibid., 7-N-11, Seton to Carroll, May 13, 1811.

[59] Ibid., 7-M-7, Seton to Carroll, Jan. 25, 1810.

[60] ASJPH, XI, 6, Seton to Wiseman, Nov. 1815.

[61] Annabelle M. Melville, *Elizabeth Bayley Seton, 1774–1821,* p. 196.

[62] ASJPH, S–F Coll., 37, Seton to Filicchi, July 1, 1814.

[63] Ibid., IV, 100, Bonaparte to Seton, n.d.

[64] Ibid., Seton to Bonaparte, n.d.

[65] Ibid., XII, 66, Seton to Bruté, Summer 1818.

[66] Ibid., XII, 31b, Seton to Bruté, Fall 1813.

[67] Ibid., S–F Coll., 114, Seton to Filicchi, Aug. 8, 1818.

[68] Ibid., XII, 68, Seton to Bruté, Dec. 26, 1816.

[69] Ibid., III, 26, *Journal* for Bruté, 1815.

[70] Ibid.

[71] Paul VI, *Homily.*

Chapter Nine
"The Embrace of Him Who Is Love"

[1] 2 Cor 12:9.

[2] ASJPH, XII, 14, Seton to Wiseman, Aug. 1818.

[3] Ibid., *Notebook, Meditations and Instructions.*

[4] AMSV, Cheverus to Seton, Aug. 11, 1818.

[5] ASJPH, S–J Coll., 114, Seton to Filicchi, Aug. 8, 1818.

[6] Ibid., *Dear Remembrances.*

7 Ibid.

8 Ibid., VI, 65, Seton to Scott, Spring 1807.

9 Ibid., XVII, 14, Dec. 13, 1803.

10 Ibid., III, 18.

11 Ibid., VII, 45, Seton to Sadler, Feb. 1812.

12 Ibid., III, 18.

13 Ibid., XVII, 14.

14 Ibid., III, 18.

15 Ibid., V, 25 (*Mulierem fortem:* Strong woman; cf. Prov 31:10–31).

16 Ibid., VII, 93, Seton to Sadler, Oct. 1812.

17 Ibid., XIII, 11, Bruté to Seton, Oct. 1812.

18 Ibid., *Notebook, Meditations and Instructions,* "Death in Desire".

19 Ibid., VI, 65, Seton to Scott, Mar.–Apr. 1807.

20 Ibid., VII, 3, Seton to Sadler, Summer 1797.

21 Ibid., X, 3a, Seton to Filicchi, June 1805.

22 Ibid.

23 Ibid., *Notebook, Meditations and Instructions.*

24 Ibid., "Meditation on the Desire of Death".

25 Ibid.

26 Ibid., *Notebook, Meditations and Instructions.*

27 Ibid., XII, 72, Seton to Bruté, Apr. 1818.

28 Ibid., 44, Seton to Bruté, n.d.

29 Ibid., 78, Seton to Bruté, Nov. 1818.

30 Ibid., XI, 25, Post to Seton, Fall 1818.

31 Ibid., I, 71, Babade to Seton, July 12, 1818.

32 AMSV, Cheverus to Seton, Aug. 11, 1818.

33 ASJPH, S–F Coll., 114, Seton to Filicchi, Aug. 8, 1818.

34 Ibid., XII, 78, Seton to Bruté, Nov. 1818.

35 AGU, 240:7, Seton to Hickey, July 2, 1820.

36 ASJPH, XII, 6.

37 Ibid., 17.

38 Ibid., 2, Bruté to Seton, Nov.–Dcc. 1820.

39 Ibid., 12b.

BIBLIOGRAPHY

Archives

Archives of St. Joseph's Provincial House, Emmitsburg, Maryland. Original letters and papers: Elizabeth Bayley Seton Letters and Papers; William Magee Seton Letters; Seton Children Letters and Papers; Seton Family Letters; Filicchi Letters; Post Letters; Sadler Letters; Scott Letters; Babade Letters and Papers; Bruté Letters and Papers; Carroll Letters; Cheverus Letters; Dubois Letters and Papers; Dubourg Letters; Matignon Letters; Tisserant Letters; Weis Letters; Wiseman Letters; Miscellaneous Letters and Papers.

Archives of the Archdiocese of Baltimore, Baltimore, Maryland; Georgetown University, Washington, District of Columbia; Mount Saint Mary's College, Emmitsburg, Maryland; and the Sisters of Charity of St. Elizabeth, Convent, New Jersey. Copies of letters and papers: Elizabeth Bayley Seton Letters and Papers; Seton Family Letters; Bruté Letters and Papers; Carroll Letters; Cheverus Letters; Dubois Letters; Dubourg Letters; David Letters; Filicchi Letters.

Archives of the Daughters of Charity, Paris, France. Original letters and papers: Labouré Papers.

Archives of the Daughters of Charity, St. Louis, Missouri. Original letters and papers: Filicchi Letters.

Archives of the Sisters of Charity of Mount Saint Vincent-on-Hudson, New York and the Sisters of Charity of Cincinnati, Ohio. Photostats of original letters and papers: Elizabeth Bayley Seton Letters; Seton Children Letters; Seton Family Letters; Carroll Letters; Cheverus Letters; Dubois Letters; David Letters; Filicchi Letters; Miscellaneous Letters and Papers.

199

Archives of the University of Notre Dame, Notre Dame, Indiana. Original letters and papers: Seton Family Letters; Egan Letters.

Other Sources

Abelly, Louis. *La Vie du Vénérable Serviteur de Dieu, Vincent de Paul.* 3 vols. Paris, 1664.

Anglin, Thomas Francis. "The Eucharistic Fast". *The Catholic University of America Canon Law Studies,* no. 124. Washington, 1941.

Baunard, Msgr. Louis. *La Vénérable Louise de Marillac.* Paris, 1898.

Bayley, James Roosevelt. *Memoirs of the Rt. Rev. Simon Wm. Gabriel Bruté, D.D., First Bishop of Vincennes.* New York, 1861.

Bedoyère, M. de la. *François de Sales.* London, 1960.

St. Bernard of Clairvaux. "Sermo in dom. infra oct. Assumptionis". *Opera Omnia,* Edit. Cisterc. 5, 1968, 273–74.

Bernardin, Joseph. *Statement on Canonization of St. Elizabeth Ann Seton.* Rome, Sept. 14, 1975.

Bremond, Henri. *Histoire Litteraire du Sentiment Religieux.* 12 vols. Paris, 1916–38.

Broglie, Prince Emmanuel de. *The Life of Blessed Louise de Marillac, Co-Foundress of the Sisters of Charity of Saint Vincent de Paul,* tr. by Joseph Leonard, C.M. London, 1933.

Calvet, Jean. *St. Vincent de Paul,* tr. by Lancelot C. Sheppard. New York, 1948.

——. *Louise de Marillac,* tr. by G. F. Pullen. New York, 1959.

Carson, Mary. "Let's Speed up Canonization". *The Catholic Standard and Times,* Philadelphia, Jan. 30, 1975.

Chaigne, Louis. *St. Vincent de Paul,* tr. by Rosemary Sheed. New York, 1962.

Codicis Juris Canonicis Fontes.

Common Rules of the Daughters of Charity. Paris, 1658, 1954.

Constitutiones et Statuta Congregationis Missionis. Romae, 1984.

Coste, Pierre, C.M. *The Life and Works of Saint Vincent de Paul.* 3 vols., tr. by Joseph Leonard, C.M. Westminster, 1952.

Daniel-Rops, Henri. *Monsieur Vincent.* Biographie illustré par Jean Servel, Maquette et photos de René Perrin. Lyon, 1959.

———. *Monsieur Vincent, The Story of St. Vincent de Paul,* tr. by Julie Kernan. New York, 1961.

Daughters of Charity of Saint Vincent de Paul, Constitutions and Statutes. Paris, 1983.

de Caussade, Jean-Pierre. *Abandonment to Divine Providence.* St. Louis, 1921.

De Lehen. *The Way of Interior Peace,* tr. by James Brucker. New York, 1888.

de Marillac, St. Louise. *Correspondance, Meditations, Pensées, Avis.* Paris, 1961.

de Paul, St. Vincent. *Saint Vincent de Paul, Correspondance, Entretiens, Documents.* Tomes XIII, edition publiée et annotée par Pierre Coste, Prêtre de la Mission. Paris, 1920.

———. *Entretiens Spirituels aux Missionaires.* Textes reunis et présenté par Andre Dodin, C.M. Paris, 1960.

de Sales, Francis. *Introduction to the Devout Life,* tr. by John K. Ryan. Garden City, New York, 1955.

Dictionnaire de Theologie Catholique. "Baptême dans L'Eglise Anglicane", vol. 2. Paris, 1922.

Dirvin, Joseph I., C.M. *St. Catherine Labouré of the Miraculous Medal.* New York, 1958; Rockford, 1986.

———. *Mrs. Seton, Foundress of the American Sisters of Charity.* New York, 1962, 1975.

———. *Louise de Marillac.* New York, 1970.

Giordani, Igino. *St. Vincent de Paul, Servant of the Poor,* tr. by Thomas J. Tobin. Milwaukee, 1961.

Giraud, Victor. *St. Vincent de Paul,* tr. by Joseph Leonard, C.M. Dublin, 1955.

Grou, J. N. *Spiritual Maxims,* tr. by Theodore Baker. London, 1922.

Guardini, Romano. *The Lord,* tr. by Elinor Castendyk Briefs. Chicago, 1954.

Kelly, Ellen M., Ph.D. *Elizabeth Seton's Two Bibles, Her Notes and Markings.* Huntington, 1977.

Lavedan, Henri Léon Emile. *The Heroic Life of St. Vincent de Paul,* tr. by Helen Younger Chase. London and New York, 1929.

Laverty, Sister Rose Maria. *Loom of Mercy Threads: The English and French Influences on the Character of Elizabeth Ann Bayley Seton.* New York, 1940.

Leen, Edward. *In the Likeness of Christ.* New York, 1940.

Leen, James. *By Jacob's Well, A Planned Retreat,* tr. by Edward Leen. New York, 1940.

Lovat, Alice Mary (Weld-Blundell) Fraser, Baroness. *Life of the Venerable Louise de Marillac (Mademoiselle Le Gras), Foundress of the Company of Sisters of Charity of St. Vincent de Paul.* London, 1916.

McLaughlin, Arthur. *St. Vincent de Paul, Servant of the Poor.* Milwaukee, 1965.

Marmion, Dom Columba. *Christ the Life of the Soul,* tr. by a Nun of Tyburn Convent. St. Louis, 1925.

——. *Christ the Ideal of the Monk,* tr. by a Nun of Tyburn Convent. London, 1926.

Matt, Leonard von. *St. Vincent de Paul,* tr. by Emma Crawford. Chicago, 1960.

Maturin, B. *Self-Knowledge and Self-Discipline.* New York, 1922.

Maynard, Theodore. *Apostle of Charity, the Life of St. Vincent de Paul.* New York, 1939.

The New American Bible. New York and Toronto, 1970.

Paul VI. *Homily.* Canonization of St. Elizabeth Ann Seton. Rome, Sept. 14, 1975.

——. *Remarks to the American Bishops.* Rome, Sept. 15, 1975.

Purcell, Mary. *The World of Monsieur Vincent.* New York, 1963.

Seton, Elizabeth. *Elizabeth Seton, Selected Writings,* ed. by Ellen Kelly and Annabelle Melville. New York and Mahwah, N.J., 1987.

Sheedy, J.P., C.M. *Untrodden Paths: The Social Apostolate of St. Louise de Marillac.* London, 1958.

The Sixteen Documents of Vatican II and the Instruction on the Liturgy with Commentaries by the Council Fathers, commentaries by the Council Fathers compiled by the Rev. J. L. Gonzalez, S.S.P., and the Daughters of St. Paul, NCWC translation. Boston, n.d.

Souvay, Charles L. "Questions Anent Mother Seton's Conversion", *The Catholic Historical Review,* vol. 5 (July–Oct. 1919): 223ff.

Stopp, Elizabeth. *Madame de Chantal, Portrait of a Saint.* Westminster, 1963.

Tanquery, Adolphe. *The Spiritual Life, a Treatise on Ascetical and Mystical Theology,* tr. by Herman Branderis. Tournai and Baltimore, 1930.

——. *Synopsis Theologiae Dogmaticae Fundamentalis.* 3 vols. Paris, Tournai and Rome, 1937.

St. Teresa of Avila. *The Life of St. Teresa of Jesus of the Order of Our Lady of Carmel Written by Herself,* tr. by David Lewis, ed. by Benedict Zimmerman. Westminster, 1933.

St. Thérèse of Lisieux. *Autobiography of St. Thérèse of Lisieux,* the complete and authorized text of "L'Histoire d'une Âme", newly translated by Ronald Knox. New York, 1958.

Thompson, Francis. *Poems of Francis Thompson,* rev. ed., ed. with biographical and textual notes by the Rev. Terence L. Connolly, S.J., Ph.D. New York and London, 1941.

Vatican Council II, the Conciliar and Post Conciliar Documents. Austin Flannery, O.P., general editor. Collegeville, Minn., 1975.

White, Charles I. *Life of Mrs. Eliza A. Seton.* Baltimore, 1853.

Woodgate, M. V. *Saint Vincent de Paul.* Westminster, 1958.

Wright, John Cardinal. *Address.* Catacomb of St. Callistus, Rome, Sept. 15, 1975.

INDEX

Abraham, Elizabeth's faith compared to that of, 36

Apostolates: holiness and good works expressed in, 113; the results of vocations, 113; Elizabeth's flowed from her two essential vocations, 113; seeds of Elizabeth's education apostolate in Protestant days, 132–33

Aridity, Elizabeth suffers, 108ff.

Augustine, St., on Mary and the Church, 165

Babade, Father Pierre: Sisters forbidden to confess to, 46; applies Psalm of "barren woman" to Elizabeth, 59; directs conversion of Harriet Seton, 125; prophesies Elizabeth's religious vocation, 127; writes to Elizabeth concerning her approaching death, 177

Baptism, no evidence of rebaptism when Elizabeth entered the Church, 161–62

Baragazzi, Father Nicóla (brother of Amabilia Filicchi), Elizabeth impressed at family wedding performed by, 69

Bayley, Barclay (half brother of Elizabeth Ann Seton), reneges on engagement to marry Harriet Seton, 125

Bayley, Catherine (Kitty) (sister of Elizabeth Ann Seton), Elizabeth at death of, 21, 170

Bayley, Catherine Charlton (mother of Elizabeth Ann Seton): Elizabeth's longing for her as a child, 21; her influence on Elizabeth, 22

Bayley, Charlotte Amelia Barclay (stepmother of Elizabeth Ann Seton), teaches Elizabeth the twenty-second Psalm, 22

Bayley, Dr. Richard (father of Elizabeth Ann Seton), offered to God by daughter, 26

Bayley, William LeConte (brother of Dr. Richard Bayley and uncle of Elizabeth Ann Seton), Elizabeth's piety while living with, 21

Benediction of the Blessed Sacrament: Elizabeth recalls "mystery" of, 73; described for Cecilia Seton by Elizabeth, 75; Elizabeth rejoices in nightly, 133

Berchmans, St. John, his avowal of the common life as the greatest mortification, 97

208

THE SOUL OF ELIZABETH SETON

Charity, opposed by self-love,
says Elizabeth, 56
Charlton, the Reverend Richard
(grandfather of Elizabeth Ann
Seton), his influence on
Elizabeth, 22
Chastity, virtue present in the
rightful desire for death, 175
Cheerfulness, prepares the soul
for true piety, according to
Elizabeth, 61–62
Cheverus, Bishop John: urges
perseverance in prayer on
Elizabeth, 63; prophesies religious vocation of Elizabeth,
127; gives Elizabeth final push
into the Church, 158–59;
believed in the validity of
Anglican baptism, 161–62;
writes to Elizabeth on her
approaching death, 177
Church: Elizabeth's faith and
love towards, 37; Elizabeth's
love of the Will of God a gift
to, 41; selects Elizabeth's conference on the Will of God as
reading for her feast, 51;
enjoins Presence of God on
novices, 53; the Mass and
Eucharist the heart of, 65;
Elizabeth sees Our Lady as a
gift to the, 83; Father Tisserant
encourages Elizabeth in practices of the, 95–96; names St.
Vincent de Paul and St. Louise
de Marillac as special pat-
ronesses, 132; recognized
Elizabeth's mission to the poor
at canonization, 132; the

Catholic school the bulwark
of the Church in America,
134; the core of Elizabeth's life
and holiness, 151; Elizabeth and
the Episcopal church, 151–52;
Elizabeth and mystery of the
Church, 152; Elizabeth's comments on the lack of perception of a true Church, 152–54;
Wright Post's bewilderment
over "Church of the
Apostles", 153; Filicchis intro-
duce Elizabeth to the, 154ff.;
Elizabeth's attraction to
Catholic practices sweetens her
first approach to the, 155;
Elizabeth perceives the lowliness of the, 156; Vatican Council II lauds the lowliness of the,
156; Elizabeth accepts the true,
158ff.; Elizabeth received into
the, 158–59; Elizabeth attests
to the infallible teaching of
the, 159; Elizabeth's loyalty
and submission to the, 159–60;
Elizabeth's joy in the
sacramental life of the, 160–62;
contemporary misconceptions
of the, 162ff.; Vatican Council II's teaching on the, 162ff.;
St. Augustine discusses Mary
and the, 165; Elizabeth's
humility before the mystery of
the, 165ff.; Elizabeth urges her
sisters to be children of the,
165; Elizabeth's submission to
not confining, 165–66; mutual
love of Elizabeth and the,
167–68; Elizabeth perceives

Union with God: Elizabeth's joy in, 54ff.; simplicity of, 55–56; self-love an obstacle to, says Elizabeth, 56; served by cheerfulness, according to Elizabeth, 61–62; Elizabeth's desire for sacramental union as a Protestant, 65–67; Elizabeth seeks, at last Mass in Italy, 70; Elizabeth urges union with Jesus' love of the Father in holy Communion, 76–77; suffering a way to, 99, 100; the interior life and, 105; Elizabeth in unitive way accepts habitual sadness of soul, 110

Vatican Council II: and other churches and religions, 151; and the lowliness and poverty of the Church, 156 and its teaching on the Church, 162ff.
Vincentian Fathers, Elizabeth rejoices at arrival of, 113
Vocation(s): a call to apostolates, 113; Elizabeth's two essential, 113; Elizabeth's children have priority over religious, 117–18; early hints of Elizabeth's religious, 123ff.; Elizabeth's conversion a step towards, 125ff.; Elizabeth's religious prophesied, 125–127; Elizabeth called to Baltimore, 126; mutual attraction of Samuel Cooper and Elizabeth a momentary distraction from theirs, 126; Elizabeth's embraces the poor and Catholic education, 127ff.; the seeds of Elizabeth's educational calling sown in Protestant days, 132–33

Voltaire, François Marie Arouet, his rationalism rampant in Elizabeth's lifetime, 51–52

Weis, George: Elizabeth confides love of God's Will to, 48–49; Elizabeth urges cheerfulness on, 62; Elizabeth urges the Cross on, 99ff.; Elizabeth sees his name on her crucifix, 99; Elizabeth united to his suffering, 99–100; Elizabeth suggests, in spiritual jest, that Cecilia Seton is cause of his troubles, 101
White, Sister Rose: proposed by Father David to replace Elizabeth, 46; describes sufferings of first year of Philadelphia mission, 98–99
Widows' Society in New York, Elizabeth a co-founder of, 128
Will of God: St. Elizabeth Ann Seton's love of, 35; this love revealed to Mrs. Scott, 35; submission to and love of discussed, 35; role of faith in, 35–36; revealed to Elizabeth by contradictions, 39ff.; Elizabeth's docility to, a gift to the Church, 41; and the establishment of the Sisterhood, 41–43; Elizabeth accepts position of authority as, 43–45; early crisis in

DATE DUE